Ultimate Sweet
Treats

Ultimate Sweet
Treats

LONDON, NEW YORK, MUNICH,
MELBOURNE AND DELHI

Senior Editor Catherine Saunders
Senior Designer Lisa Crowe
Editors Heather Scott, Julia March, Elizabeth Noble
Designers Dan Bunyan, Justin Greenwood,
Lynne Moulding, Thelma-Jane Robb
Home Economists Katharine Ibbs, Denise Smart
Assistant Home Economists Fergal Connolly,
Lisa Harrison, Sarah Tildesley
Consultant Nicola Graimes

Designer David McDonald
Production Controller Sarah Hughes

Publishing Managers Simon Beecroft, Cynthia O'Neill Collins
Category Publisher Alex Allan/Siobhan Williamson
Production Amy Bennett, Rochelle Talary

THE ULTIMATE CHILDREN'S COOKBOOK
Senior Designer Philip Letsu
Designer Johnny Pau
Senior Editor Julie Ferris

First published in Great Britain in 2010 by
Dorling Kindersley Limited,
80 Strand, London, WC2R 0RL

This edition produced for The Book People,
Hall Wood Avenue, Haydock,
St. Helens WA11 9UL

Contains content from *Ultimate Children's Cookbook* (2009),
The Children's Baking Book (2009)

2 4 6 8 10 9 7 5 3 1

© 2010 Dorling Kindersley Ltd.

A CIP catalogue record for this book is available from the British Library.

ISBN: 978-1-4053-6171-2

Reproduced by Media Development and Printing Ltd., UK
Printed and bound in China by L Rex Printing Company

Discover more at
www.dk.com

Contents

Introduction

It is so satisfying to eat food you have cooked yourself, and baking is one of the most enjoyable methods of cooking. Baking uses lots of great techniques and delicious ingredients and, best of all, it fills your kitchen with the most wonderful smells! You can bake for special occasions or just for everyday eating.

Getting Started

1. Read the recipe thoroughly before you begin.

2. Wash your hands, tie your hair back (if necessary) and put on your apron.

3. Gather all the ingredients and equipment you need before you begin.

4. Start baking!

Be sensible! Take extra care when you see this symbol because hot ovens, cookers or sharp knives are involved.

You might need to ask an adult for help if you see this symbol. But don't be shy – ask for help whenever you think you need it!

Safe Baking

Cooking is great fun but with heat and sharp objects around, you must always take care to be safe and sensible.

- Use oven gloves when handling hot pans, trays or bowls.
- Don't put hot pans or trays directly onto the work surface – use a heatproof trivet, mat, rack or board.
- When you are stirring food on the cooker, grip the handle firmly to steady the pan.
- When cooking on the stove, turn the pan handles to the side (away from the heat and the front) so that you are less likely to knock them over.
- Take extra care when you see the red warning triangle on a step.
- Ask an adult for help when you see the green warning triangle.

Kitchen Hygiene

After safety, cleanliness is the most important thing to be aware of in the kitchen. Here are a few simple hygiene rules for you to follow:

- Always wash your hands before you start baking.
- Wash all fruit and vegetables.
- Keep your cooking area clean and have a cloth handy to clean up any spills.
- Store cooked and raw food separately.
- Always check the use-by date on all ingredients. Do not use them if the date has passed.
- Keep fresh foods such as eggs in the refrigerator until you need them and always take care to cook them properly.

Did You Know?

Humans are the only creatures on Earth that eat cooked food. All other creatures (except for domesticated animals) eat their food raw and unprocessed.

Using the Recipes

There is a lot of information to take in so here's how to get the most out of the recipes. You'll find simple instructions, tips, delicious variations and mouthwatering recipes.

Check out useful cooking tips.

Collect all the ingredients and equipment you need before you start.

This row tells you how much time to leave for preparation and cooking and how many cakes, biscuits etc. you can expect to make.

Step-by-step pictures and text guide you through the recipes.

Some of the recipes can be adapted to make different flavours.

Cupcakes and Cakes

Both Cupcakes and Cakes use the same baking methods but cupcakes are individual little cakes. They are a great favourite at parties and for special occasions.

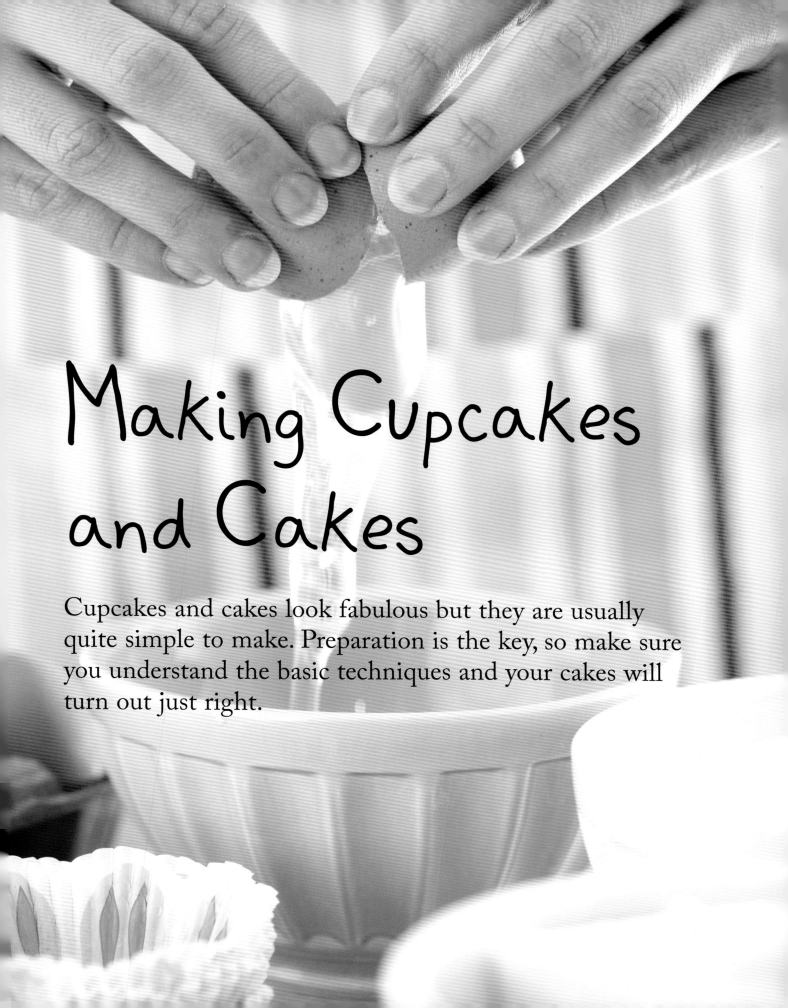

Making Cupcakes and Cakes

Cupcakes and cakes look fabulous but they are usually quite simple to make. Preparation is the key, so make sure you understand the basic techniques and your cakes will turn out just right.

Creaming

Mixing together sugar and butter is called creaming. If your butter is at room temperature you will find it much easier to mix.

Correct temperature

It is very important to use your ingredients at the correct temperature. Eggs should be at room temperature, otherwise they might curdle.

Testing a cake with a skewer

To test whether a cake is cooked properly, stick a skewer or knife in it. It will come out clean if the cake is cooked. If it has cake mixture on it, put the cake back in the oven for 5 minutes.

How to line a cake tin

1. Put the cake tin on top of some baking paper and draw round the bottom with a pencil or pen.

2. Cut out the shape with scissors and place the baking paper inside the tin.

Folding

Folding is a gentle method of mixing that keeps a cake light and airy. Use a metal spoon to fold the mixture over itself, instead of stirring it in a circle.

Pretty Cupcakes

Cook these pretty cakes and decorate with pastel colour icings, sweets or crystallised flowers. Stack in a tower as an alternative way to celebrate a birthday party or get-together.

These cakes are easy and quick to make, and even quicker to eat!

Helpful Hint

These cakes can be made the day before and stored in an airtight container.

Ingredients

Cakes:

- 150g (5½oz) unsalted butter, softened
- 150g (5½oz) caster sugar
- 150g (5½oz) self-raising flour
- 3 medium eggs, whisked
- 2.5ml (½tsp) vanilla extract

sugar

Icing and decoration:

- 225g (8oz) icing sugar, sifted
- 30 to 45ml (2 to 3tbsp) hot water
- 3 different food colourings
- Edible crystallised flowers, sugar strands, hundreds and thousands, or sweets

eggs

Equipment

- 2 x12 bun tins
- 20 paper cases
- 2 mixing bowls
- wooden spoon
- 2 metal spoons
- cooling rack
- knife
- 3 small mixing bowls

bun tin

mixing bowl

1 Line 2 x 12 bun tins with 20 paper cases. Preheat the oven to 180°C, 350°F, gas mark 4.

2 Place the butter, sugar, self-raising flour, eggs, and vanilla extract in a bowl and beat with a wooden spoon until pale and creamy.

3 Divide between the paper cases. Bake for 15 minutes until golden and just firm. Cool in the tin for 5 minutes, then transfer to a cooling rack to cool.

4 Trim any pointed tops to make a flat surface.

5 Place the icing in a large bowl, gradually beat in sufficient water to give a smooth thick icing, which coats the back of a spoon.

6 Transfer the icing mixture to 3 individual bowls and add a few drops of food colouring to each. Spoon onto the cakes and top with decorations. Allow to set.

Raspberry Cupcakes

This recipe teams white chocolate with fresh raspberries to make a wonderful fresh-tasting but rich cupcake. Always wash and dry the raspberries well before using.

Ingredients

Self-raising flour

- 225g (8oz) unsalted butter, softened
- 225g (8oz) caster sugar
- 225g (8oz) self-raising flour
- 1 tsp baking powder
- 4 eggs
- 3 tbsp ground almonds
- 150g (5 ½oz) raspberries, plus 18 extra, to decorate
- 175g (6oz) white chocolate, plus extra, grated, to decorate

Raspberries

Caster sugar

Eggs

Unsalted butter

Equipment

- 2 x 12 bun tins
- Wooden Spoon
- 18 paper cases
- Large mixing bowl
- Electric or hand whisk
- Metal spoon
- Oven gloves
- Cooling rack
- Small mixing bowl
- Sieve
- Teaspoon

Wooden spoon

1 Preheat the oven to 180°C (350°F, gas mark 4). Line the bun tin with paper baking cases.

2 Place the butter, caster sugar, flour, baking powder, and eggs in a large mixing bowl and beat with an electric hand whisk for 2–3 minutes, or until well combined. Stir in the almonds and raspberries, then spoon the mixture into the paper baking cases and bake for 18 minutes, or until risen and golden brown. Place on a wire rack to cool completely.

3 Put the white chocolate in a bowl and place it over a pan of barely simmering water until the chocolate has melted. Drizzle over the top of the cup cakes. Decorate each one with grated white chocolate and a raspberry.

Vanilla Cupcakes

Coloured buttercream icing and simple decorations transform these easy cupcakes into real family favourites. They look great decorated with tiny metallic balls.

Ingredients

Caster sugar

- 225g (8oz) unsalted butter, softened
- 225g (8oz) caster sugar
- 225g (8oz) self-raising flour
- 1 tsp baking powder
- 4 eggs

Butter

- 1 tsp pure vanilla extract
- Buttercream icing, coloured pale pink and yellow with food colouring
- Pink metallic balls, to decorate (optional)

Eggs

Self-raising flour

Equipment

- 2 x 12 bun tins
- Woodenspoon and spatula
- 18 paper cases
- Large mixing bowl
- Electric or hand whisk
- Metal spoon
- Oven gloves
- Cooling rack
- Small mixing bowl
- Sieve
- Piping bag

Electric whisk

Piping the icing

Make a simple piping bag as shown on page 137. For finer piping, use a cloth piping bag with a nozzle tip. Twist the bag around the nozzle.

Turn the bag inside out and scoop icing into it with a spatula. When you have enough, untwist the nozzle and squeeze the bag to begin piping.

1 Preheat the oven to 180°C (350°F, gas mark 4). Line a bun tray with 18–20 paper baking cases.

2 Place the butter, sugar, flour, baking powder, eggs, and vanilla extract in a large mixing bowl and beat with an electric whisk for 2–3 minutes, or until light and fluffy.

3 Spoon into the paper baking cases and bake for 18 minutes, or until risen and golden brown. Transfer to a wire rack to cool completely.

Variation
Use more than two colourings to create different effects for a special occasion. You could also decorate with different coloured metal balls.

Orange and Lemon Cupcakes

The orange and lemon zest makes these cupcakes taste fresh and tangy and the different colours of icing make them look scrumptious. Decorate with sugar strands or sugar stars.

Ingredients

- 200g (7oz) butter
- 200g (7oz) caster sugar
- 3 large eggs
- 200g (7oz) self-raising flour
- Finely grated zest and juice of 1 large orange
- Finely grated zest of 1 lemon (from the lemon used for the icing)

Butter

Eggs

For the icing

- 50g (2oz) butter
- 125g (4oz) icing sugar
- juice of 1 lemon
- Few drops of natural yellow food colouring
- Few drops of natural orange food colouring

Lemon

Equipment

- 1 × 12 bun tin
- 12 paper cases
- Large mixing bowl
- Electric or hand whisk
- Wooden spoon
- Metal spoon
- Oven gloves
- Cooling rack
- Small mixing bowl
- Sieve
- Teaspoon

Oven gloves

1 Preheat the oven to 180ºC (350ºF, gas mark 4). Line a 12-cup deep-sized bun tin with paper cases.

2 Whisk together the butter, sugar, eggs, flour, and orange and lemon zest until pale and fluffy, then add the orange juice a little at a time until the mixture drops off the whisk easily.

3 Divide the mixture into the paper cases evenly and bake for about 25–30 minutes, until lightly golden brown, risen, and springy when you touch them. Leave to cool in the tin for a few minutes before sitting them on a wire rack to cool completely.

4 To make the icing, beat the butter and icing sugar together, then stir in the lemon juice. Divide the mixture in two and spoon one half of it into another bowl. Mix a few drops of yellow colouring into one half (until you have the colour you want), and a few drops of orange into the other half.

5 Spread the icing over the cakes then sprinkle with sugar strands or arrange sugar stars carefully on top.

Vanilla Cupcakes with Chocolate Icing

These cupcakes are a delicious combination of vanilla and chocolate. Use milk or dark chocolate for the shavings.

Ingredients

- 125g (4 ½oz) butter, at room temperature
- 125g (4 ½oz) caster sugar
- 2 large eggs
- 125g (4 ½oz) self-raising flour, sifted
- 1 tsp vanilla extract
- 1 tbsp milk, if necessary

Self-raising flour

For the icing

- 100g (3 ½oz) icing sugar
- 15g (½oz) cocoa powder (optional)
- 100g (3 ½oz) butter, at room temperature
- few drops of vanilla extract
- 25g (scant 1oz) milk or dark chocolate, shaved with a vegetable peeler (optional)

Chocolate

Equipment

- 1 ×12 bun tin
- 12 paper cases
- Large mixing bowl
- Electric or hand whisk
- Wooden spoon
- Metal spoon
- Oven gloves
- Cooling rack
- Small mixing bowl
- Sieve
- Teaspoon

Bun tin

Wooden spoon

1 Preheat the oven to 190°C (375°F, gas mark 5). Line the bun tin with cupcake cases. Place the butter and sugar in a bowl, and whisk with an electric hand whisk until pale and fluffy. Beat in the eggs one at a time, adding a little of the flour after adding each one.

2 Add the vanilla extract and then the rest of the flour, and mix well until smooth. The mixture should drop easily off the beaters. If it doesn't, stir in the milk.

3 Spoon the mixture into the cupcake cases. Bake for 20 minutes, or until the cupcakes have risen and are golden, and firm to the touch. Transfer the cupcakes to a wire rack to cool.

4 To make the icing, sift the icing sugar and cocoa powder (if using), into a bowl, add the butter and the vanilla extract, and whisk with an electric hand whisk until the mixture is light and fluffy. Ice the cupcakes, giving the top of each one a swirly design. Scatter over the chocolate shavings, if using.

Variation

For lemon cupcakes, instead of chocolate, add zest of 1/2 lemon to the cake mixture and 1–2 tablespoons lemon juice to the icing. Leave out the cocoa powder.

Carrot Cupcakes

The grated carrots make these individual cakes perfectly moist and the yummy cream cheese frosting makes a deliciously tangy topping.

Ingredients

- 175g (6oz) butter (softened)
- 175g (6oz) caster sugar
- 175g (6oz) self-raising flour
- 2tsp mixed spice
- 2 large eggs
- Grated zest of 1 orange and 1tbsp juice
- 2 medium carrots (peeled and coarsely grated)

Carrots

- 50g (2oz) brazil or walnuts toasted and chopped (optional)

Frosting

- 200g (7oz) light cream cheese
- 2tbsp icing sugar
- 1tbsp orange juice
- 2tsp grated orange zest

Orange

Orange juice

Equipment

- 2 x 12 bun tins
- 18 paper cases
- Large mixing bowl
- Electric or hand whisk
- Sieve
- Dessert spoon
- Oven gloves
- Cooling rack
- Wooden spoon
- Medium bowl

Bun tin

Electric whisk

1 Preheat the oven to 180°C, (350°F, gas mark 4). Place 18 paper cases in a bun tin. Most bun tins only have 12 holes so you may have to use two tins or cook your cakes in batches.

2 In a large mixing bowl, beat together the butter and sugar until they become pale and fluffy. Use an electric whisk if you have one. If not, then use a hand whisk.

3 Sift the flour and mixed spice into the bowl. Then add the eggs, orange juice and zest. Whisk together until all the ingredients are completely combined.

4 Stir the grated carrots and nuts (if you are using them) into the mixing bowl. Divide the mixture equally between the 18 paper cases using a dessert spoon.

5 Bake for 18–20 minutes in the middle of the oven until risen and golden brown. Remove from the oven using the oven gloves, and place on a cooling rack to cool completely.

6 Beat together all the frosting ingredients with a wooden spoon. Spread the frosting over the cooled cakes and decorate the cupcakes with extra orange zest.

Chocolate Cupcakes

One of the best things about cupcakes is that everybody has their own little cake. Chocolate is always a popular flavour and really easy topping to make.

Variation

It is easy to change the look of these cupcakes by decorating with any of your favourite toppings. Use chocolate beans, or sugar strands and sugar flowers for a more colourful look.

Ingredients

Self-raising flour

- 225g (8oz) unsalted butter, softened
- 225g (8oz) caster sugar
- 225g (8oz) self-raising flour
- 1 tsp baking powder
- 4 eggs
- 2 tbsp cocoa powder
- 100g (3½oz) chocolate chips
- 175g (6oz) plain chocolate
- flaked chocolate, to decorate

Chocolate

Equipment

- 2 x 12 bun tins
- 18 paper cases
- Large mixing bowl
- Electric or hand whisk
- Wooden spoon
- Metal spoon
- Oven gloves
- Cooling rack
- Small mixing bowl
- Sieve
- Teaspoon

Bun tin

Sieve

1 Preheat the oven to 180°C (350°F, gas mark 4). Line a bun tray with 18–20 paper baking cases.

2 Place the butter, caster sugar, flour, baking powder, eggs, and cocoa powder in a large mixing bowl and beat with an electric whisk for 2–3 minutes, or until mixture into light and fluffy.

3 Stir in the chocolate chips, spoon the mixture into the paper cases, and bake for 18 minutes, or until well risen. Transfer to a wire rack to cool.

4 Melt the chocolate in a bowl over a pan of simmering water, then spoon over the top of the cooled cup cakes. Decorate with flaked chocolate. Leave until set.

Lime and Coconut Cupcakes

Give classic cupcakes a makeover with mouthwatering coconut and refreshing lime.

Variation
Instead of lime zest and juice, add 2tsp vanilla extract in Step 2. Stir a little vanilla extract and water in Step 5 instead of lime zest and juice.

Ingredients

- 125g (4oz) butter (softened)
- 125g (4oz) caster sugar
- Finely grated zest and juice of 2 limes
- 2 medium eggs
- 150g (5oz) self-raising flour
- 1tsp baking powder
- 50g (2oz) sweetened and tenderised or desiccated coconut

For the icing

- Finely grated zest and juice of 1 lime
- 175g (6oz) icing sugar
- Few drops green food colouring (optional)
- 2tbsp sweetened and tenderised or desiccated coconut

Sugar

Flour

Equipment

Bun tin

- 2 ×12 hole bun tins
- 18 paper cases
- Large mixing bowl
- Electric or hand whisk
- Metal spoon
- Oven gloves
- Cooling rack
- Small mixing bowl
- Sieve
- Teaspoon

1 Preheat the oven to 180°C (350°F, gas mark 4). Line the bun tins with 18 paper cases. Use two 12-hole bun tins if you don't have a 6-hole tin or cook the cupcakes in batches.

2 In a large mixing bowl, whisk the butter, sugar and lime zest together using an electric or hand whisk until they are light and fluffy. Whisk in the eggs and lime juice.

3 Using a metal spoon, fold the flour, baking powder and coconut into the butter and sugar mixture. Divide the mixture between the paper cases. They should be about ⅔ full.

4 Cook the cupcakes in the oven for 15–20 minutes until well risen and golden (cook them on the top shelf if you are cooking in batches). Transfer to a cooling rack and allow to cool.

5 Place ⅔ of the lime zest (saving some for decoration) and lime juice in a bowl and sift over the icing sugar. Stir until the icing is smooth, adding a little green colouring if you are using it.

6 Use a teaspoon to drizzle the icing over the tops of the cooled cupcakes and sprinkle over the coconut. Add the saved curls of lime zest to decorate.

Cakes

Baking cakes can be a lot of fun and most cakes will keep in an airtight container for several days.

Passion Cake

With no creaming or whisking, this is a deliciously simple cake recipe. Carrots give the cake a light and moist texture, as well as providing essential nutrients.

Helpful Hints

To test if the cake is cooked, insert a metal skewer into its centre. If it comes out clean, without cake mixture sticking to it, the cake is ready to take out of the oven.

Decorate the cake with slivers of orange peel.

Ingredients

- butter (for greasing)
- 125g (4½ oz) wholemeal self-raising flour
- 125g (4½ oz) white self-raising flour
- 2 tsp ground mixed spice
- 250g (9oz) light muscovado sugar

self-raising wholemeal flour

- 250g (9oz) carrots (peeled and grated)
- 4 free-range eggs
- 200ml (7fl oz) sunflower oil
- 125g (4½ oz) reduced-fat cream cheese
- 1 tsp vanilla extract
- 5 tbsp unrefined icing sugar

free-range eggs

Equipment

- 20cm (8in) square cake tin
- baking paper
- sieve
- large mixing bowl
- wooden spoon
- measuring jug
- skewer
- palette knife

measuring jug

sieve

1 Preheat the oven to 180°C (350°F/Gas 4). Lightly grease a 20cm (8in) square cake tin and then carefully line the base with baking paper.

2 Sift both types of flour into a bowl, adding any bran left in the sieve. Stir in the mixed spice, sugar, and carrots until they are thoroughly combined.

3 Crack the eggs into a jug. Use a fork to lightly beat them together. Then pour the eggs into the bowl with the flour mixture.

4 Add the oil and then stir until all the ingredients are mixed together. Pour the mixture into the tin and smooth the top with the back of a spoon.

Food Facts

Not all fats are bad. Vegetable oil is a type of unsaturated fat which is a good source of energy and helps your body to absorb some vitamins.

vegetable oil

5 Bake the cake for 50 minutes until it is risen and golden. Remove it from the oven and leave to cool in the tin for 10 minutes before turning it out.

6 Carefully turn the cake out on to a cooling rack. Put the cream cheese and icing into a bowl and beat together until smooth and creamy.

7 Stir in the vanilla extract. Put the icing in the fridge for 15 minutes to harden slightly. Spead the icing over the cake and smooth using a palette knife.

Gingerbread House

For an extra surprise, fill the centre of the house with more sweets before attaching the roof.

Try making gingerbread men, women and children to live in your house.

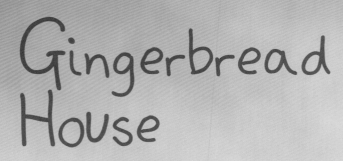

Ingredients

Dough:

- 250g (9oz) unsalted butter (softened)
- 150g (5½ oz) soft brown sugar
- 2 medium eggs, beaten
- 175ml (6floz) golden syrup
- 30ml (2tbsp) ground ginger

eggs

- 625g (1½ lb) plain flour
- 10ml (2tsp) bicarbonate of soda

For decoration:

- 1 egg white
- 225g (8oz) icing sugar (sifted)
- marshmallows, halved, for the roof and sweets of your choice

flour

Equipment

- two 18 × 10cm (7 × 4in) rectangles for the roof
- two 15 × 10cm (6 × 4in) rectangles for the sides. Add windows
- two 10cm (4in) squares for the ends, extending 7½cm (3in) from the top edge of the squares to a point. Add a door
- food processor
- cling film
- rolling pin
- baking paper
- knife
- mixing bowl
- spoon
- cooling rack

food processor

1 Place the butter and sugar in a food processor and blend until creamy. Add the eggs, golden syrup, ginger, bicarbonate of soda, and half the flour and process.

2 Add the remaining flour and process until the mixture forms a ball. Wrap in cling film and chill for 30 minutes. Meanwhile, cut out the templates.

3 Preheat the oven to 180ºC, 350ºF, gas mark 4. Roll out the dough between 2 pieces of baking paper to 5mm (¼in) thick. Use the templates to cut the dough.

4 Chill for 10 minutes, then bake for 12 minutes. Leave to cool for 2 minutes, then transfer to a cooling rack. Beat the egg white and icing sugar together.

5 Join the front and sides of the house together with a little of the icing and allow to dry. Add the back and roof in the same way. Decorate with icing and sweets.

Caramel Shortbread

Caramel shortbread is also known as millionaires' shortbread. It is more like a biscuit than a cake and is definitely for those with a sweet tooth!

Ingredients

Base:
- 50g (2oz) soft brown sugar
- 125g (4oz) butter (softened)
- 150g (5½oz) self- raising flour

Caramel topping:
- 397g (14oz) can sweetened condensed milk
- 125g (4oz) butter (diced)
- 75g (3oz) soft light brown sugar
- 50ml (2tbsp) golden syrup

Chocolate topping:
- 75g (3oz) white chocolate
- 75g (3oz) plain chocolate

chocolate

self-raising flour

Equipment

- 8 x 28cm (7 x 11in) baking tin
- baking paper
- electric whisk
- mixing bowl
- wooden spoon
- saucepan
- 2 bowls
- metal spoon

mixing bowl

saucepan

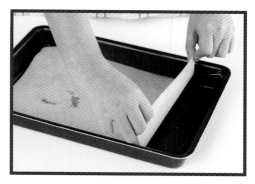

1 Preheat the oven to 180ºC, 350ºF, gas mark 4. Grease and line a 18 x 28cm (7 x 11in) tin with baking paper.

2 Cream together the butter and sugar until light and fluffy. Stir in the flour and mix until combined.

3 Press the mixture over the base of the tin and bake for 15 to 20 minutes until golden. Leave to cool.

4 Place the caramel topping ingredients in a saucepan. Place over a low heat until dissolved and bring to the boil. Continue to boil, stirring continuously, for 10 to 12 minutes.

5 Pour the caramel topping over the base. Leave to cool completely. Melt the chocolate in separate bowls over a pan of simmering water.

6 Pour the dark and white chocolate over the caramel and swirl together with the back of a spoon. Leave to set, then cut into squares.

These shortbread bites are lots of fun to make. What patterns can you create?

Banana and Pineapple Cake

This rich, moist cake is the tastiest fruit cake around! It is the perfect addition to a picnic or school lunchbox or it makes a great after-dinner treat.

Did you know?
Banana plants have been around for a long time. One of the first records dates back to Alexander the Great's conquest of India where he discovered bananas in 327 BCE!

Ingredients

self-raising wholemeal flour

bananas

- 125g (4oz) unsalted butter, cut into small pieces (plus extra for greasing)
- 5 small bananas (about 450g/1lb peeled weight)
- 75g (3oz) ready-to-eat dried pineapple
- 175g (6oz) self-raising white flour
- 50g (2oz) self-raising wholemeal flour
- 1 tsp baking powder
- pinch of salt
- 125g (4oz) unrefined caster sugar
- 2 large free-range eggs
- 50g (2oz) chopped walnuts (optional)

free-range eggs

Equipment

- 900g (2lb) loaf tin
- baking paper
- small bowl
- fork
- scissors
- sieve
- large mixing bowl
- wooden spoon

scissors

mixing bowl

loaf tin

1 Preheat the oven to 180°C (350°F/Gas 4). Trace around the loaf tin onto baking paper and cut it out. Lightly grease the tin with butter and then line.

2 Put the bananas in a bowl and mash them with a fork. Cut the pineapple into very small pieces. Set the bananas and pineapple aside.

3 Sift the flour, baking powder, and salt into a mixing bowl. Stir and then add the butter. Rub the butter into the flour mixture until it looks like fine breadcrumbs.

4 One at a time, crack the eggs into a small bowl. Lightly beat the eggs together with a fork until the white and yolk are mixed together.

Food Facts

Pineapple is great for sensitive stomach because it contains an enzyme called bromelain which is anti-inflammatory. It helps to reduce swelling and aids speedy recovery from surgery. It also aids digestion.

pineapple

5 Pour the beaten eggs into the mixing bowl, add the sugar, bananas, and pineapple and mix together. Pour the cake mixture into the prepared cake tin.

6 Make sure the mixture is level and then sprinkle over the walnuts. Cook in the centre of the oven for about 50 minutes until risen and golden.

7 Remove from the oven and place on a cooling rack for 10 minutes. Carefully turn the cooled cake out of the tin, cut into slices, and serve.

Simple Sponge Cake

This cake is wonderfully light and moist. You can also make individual fairy cakes with this recipe and decorate with your favourite toppings.

Variation
This mixture will also make 20 fairy cakes, simply divide the mixture between paper cake cases and bake for 15 minutes.

Ingredients

For the sponge
- 175g (6oz) butter (softened)
- 175g (6oz) caster sugar
- 3 medium eggs (beaten)
- 1tsp vanilla extract
- 175g (6oz) self-raising flour
- 1tsp baking powder
- 4tbsp raspberry or strawberry jam

Strawberry jam

- Icing sugar (for dusting)

For the buttercream
- 50g (2oz) butter (softened)
- 125g (4oz) icing sugar
- ½tsp vanilla extract
- 2tsp milk

Butter

Milk

Equipment
- 2 x 20cm (8") round cake tins
- Baking paper
- Large mixing bowl
- Sieve
- Electric or hand whisk
- Tablespoon
- Oven gloves
- Cooling rack
- Mixing bowl
- Wooden spoon
- Spatula

Oven gloves

1 Preheat the oven to 180°C (350°F, gas mark 4). Grease two 20cm (8") round cake tins and line each base with baking paper so that the sponge cakes don't stick.

2 Place the butter, sugar, eggs and vanilla extract in a large bowl and sift over the flour and baking powder. Using an electric or hand whisk, beat all the ingredients together until thick.

3 Divide the mixture between the two tins, levelling the tops with the back of a tablespoon. Bake in the centre of the oven for 25–30 minutes, or until risen and firm to the touch.

4 Leave the cakes to cool in the tins for a few minutes, then turn them out onto a cooling rack. Peel off the baking paper and allow the cakes to cool completely.

5 To make the buttercream filling place the butter, icing sugar, vanilla extract and milk in a mixing bowl. Beat them together with a wooden spoon until smooth and creamy.

6 Spread the flat side of one of the cakes with the jam. Spread the flat side of the other with the buttercream, then sandwich the two halves together. Dust with icing sugar.

Double Chocolate Fudge Cake

If you are a chocolate lover, you will adore this cake! The dark chocolate sponge is filled and topped with a white chocolate icing.

Ingredients

For the cake

- 175g (6oz) butter (softened)
- 175g (6oz) soft brown sugar
- 150g (5oz) self-raising flour
- 25g (1oz) cocoa powder
- 1tbsp baking powder
- ½tsp bicarbonate of soda
- 3 medium eggs (beaten)
- 100ml (3½floz) sour cream

Eggs

For the icing

- 175g (6oz) white chocolate (broken into small pieces)
- 125g (4oz) butter
- 4tbsp milk
- 200g (7oz) icing sugar

Brown sugar   Milk

To decorate: Grated chocolate, chocolate buttons and cocoa powder for dusting (optional)

Equipment

- 2 x 20cm (8") cake tins
- Baking paper
- Two large mixing bowls
- Electric or hand whisk
- Sieve
- Spatula
- Oven gloves
- Cooling rack
- Heatproof bowl
- Saucepan
- Wooden spoon
- Palette knife

Sieve

Cake tins

1 Preheat the oven to 170°C (325°F, gas mark 3). Grease and line the bases of the tins with baking paper. Place the butter and sugar in a mixing bowl and whisk together until combined.

2 Sift over the flour, cocoa powder, baking powder and bicarbonate of soda. Add the eggs and the sour cream and whisk with an electric or hand whisk until combined.

3 Divide the mixture between the two tins and level the tops. Bake for 25–30 minutes. Leave to cool slightly, then turn out onto a cooling rack. Remove the baking paper.

4 To make the icing, place the chocolate, butter and milk in a heatproof bowl over a saucepan of simmering water. Stir occasionally until the ingredients are melted and smooth.

5 Sift the icing sugar into a bowl, then pour over the melted chocolate mixture. Beat together with the whisk. Allow the icing to cool, then beat again until it forms soft peaks.

6 Use a little of the icing to sandwich the two cakes together. Spread the remaining icing over the top and sides of the cake. Decorate as desired and dust with cocoa powder.

Banana and Buttermilk Cake

This cake has a lovely crumbly texture combined with crunchy nuts and soft gooey banana. It is a great way to use up any ripe bananas.

Variation
Replace the pecan nuts with chopped walnuts or brazil nuts or just leave them out.

Ingredients

- 3 ripe bananas (broken into pieces)
- 1tsp lemon juice
- 100g (3½oz) pecan nut halves (optional)
- 100g (3½oz) butter (softened)
- 175g (6oz) soft brown sugar
- 2 medium eggs (beaten)
- 1tsp vanilla extract
- 250g (9oz) plain flour
- 1tsp salt
- 1tsp bicarbonate of soda
- 1tsp ground mixed spice
- 100ml (3½floz) buttermilk

For the topping
- 1 small banana (sliced)

Bananas

Equipment

- 900g (2lb) loaf tin
- Baking paper
- Two small bowls
- Large mixing bowl
- Electric or hand whisk
- Sieve • Fork
- Metal spoon • Oven gloves
- Aluminium foil
- Cooling rack

1 Preheat the oven to 180°C (350°F, gas mark 4). Grease and line the base of a 900g (2lb) loaf tin with baking paper. Mash the banana pieces with the lemon juice, using a fork.

2 Use your hands to break the pecan halves into small pieces into a bowl if you are adding nuts. If you don't like nuts, just leave this step out.

3 Place the butter and sugar in a large mixing bowl. Using an electric or hand whisk, beat them together until they are combined and become light and fluffy.

4 Beat in the eggs and vanilla extract, a little at a time. Stir in the banana mixture. Sift in the flour, salt, bicarbonate of soda and mixed spice and stir into the mixture with a metal spoon.

5 Stir in the buttermilk. Stir in the nuts if you are using them, saving a few. Pour the mixture into the tin and place the sliced banana on the top. Sprinkle over the saved nuts.

6 Bake in the oven for 50–60 minutes. If the cake becomes too brown, cover it with foil. Allow the cake to cool in the tin, then tip it out onto a cooling rack and remove the baking paper.

Marble Cake

Chocolate and orange cake mixtures are swirled together to make this spectacular marble-effect cake. This cake is lots of fun to make and you can change your swirling patterns every time you make it! Serve it cold or hot with custard or cream. Delicious!

Variation

Experiment by flavouring the cake with a teaspoon of vanilla or peppermint essence instead of orange.

Ingredients

- 175g (6oz) butter (softened)
- 175g (6oz) caster sugar
- 175g (6oz) self-raising flour
- 3 large eggs
- Grated zest of 1 orange
- 2tbsp orange juice
- 2tbsp cocoa powder

Sugar

Orange

Eggs

Equipment

- 20cm (8") square cake tin
- Baking paper
- Large mixing bowl
- Electric or hand whisk
- Large spoon
- Sieve
- Round-bladed knife
- Oven gloves
- Chopping board
- Sharp knife

Square cake tin

1 Preheat the oven to 180°C (350°F, gas mark 4). Grease and line the base of a 20cm (8") square cake tin with baking paper to prevent the cake from sticking.

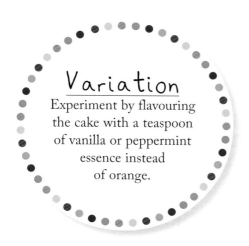

2 Place all the ingredients except the cocoa powder in a large mixing bowl. Using an electric or hand whisk, beat them all together until mixed and smooth.

3 Divide the mixture in half. Place large spoonfuls of one half of the mixture into the tin in each of the four corners and in the middle. Leave space between each spoonful.

4 Sift the cocoa powder over the remaining mixture in the bowl and whisk together until combined. Spoon the chocolate mixture into the spaces in the cake tin.

5 Gently drag a round-bladed knife through the mixtures to create a swirl effect with the brown and white mixtures. Don't overdo it, or you will mix the two colours together completely.

6 Bake the cake for 30 minutes, until well risen and springy. Allow it to cool in the tin, then remove it and peel off the baking paper. Cut it into 25 squares with a sharp knife.

Lemon Drizzle Cake

It would be hard to find a more lemony cake than this one. The luscious lemon sponge has a contrasting crusty top made by pouring the lemon syrup over the cake while it is still warm.

Chef's Tip
Adding the lemon zest when you cream the butter and sugar helps to release the oils in the zest producing a much more lemony sponge.

Ingredients

Lemon sponge

- Finely grated zest of 2 unwaxed lemons
- 200g (7oz) butter (softened)
- 200g (7oz) caster sugar
- 3 medium eggs (beaten)
- 200g (7oz) self-raising flour (sifted)

Lemons

Sugar

Unsalted butter

Syrup

- Juice 4 lemons (about 100ml (3½fl oz)
- 75g (3oz) granulated sugar

Plain Flour

Equipment

- 20cm (8") round springform cake tin
- Baking paper
- Large mixing bowl
- Electric or hand whisk
- Metal spoon
- Oven gloves
- Small mixing bowl
- Cocktail stick
- Cooling rack

Small mixing bowl

1 Preheat the oven to 180°C (350°F, gas mark 4). Butter a 20cm (8") round, springform cake tin and line the base with baking paper to prevent the cake from sticking to the tin.

2 Place the lemon zest, butter and caster sugar in a large mixing bowl and beat until the mixture is light and fluffy. You can use an electric or hand whisk.

3 Whisk in the eggs a little at a time. If the mixture starts to curdle, add 1tbsp of the flour. Use a metal spoon to fold in the flour then spoon the mixture into the prepared tin.

4 Bake the cake in the centre of the oven for 35–40 minutes. Put the lemon juice and granulated sugar in a small bowl. Leave in a warm place stirring occasionally.

5 When the cake has risen, golden and shrinking from the tin, remove it from the oven and prick all over with a cocktail stick about 20 times.

6 Drizzle the juice over the cake slowly. It will leave a crust as it sinks in. Allow the cake to cool in the tin for 10 minutes, then carefully transfer it to a cooling rack.

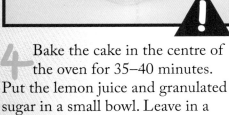

Blueberry and Sour Cream Cake

Adding sour cream makes this pretty cake wonderfully moist and creamy. It can be decorated with fresh blueberries for an extra burst of fruity flavour!

Ingredients

For the cake
- 75g (3oz) butter (softened)
- 250g (9oz) caster sugar
- 284ml pot sour cream
- 2 medium eggs
- 2tsp vanilla extract
- 300g (11oz) self-raising flour
- 1tsp baking powder
- 225g (8oz) blueberries

For the frosting
- 200g (7oz) cream cheese
- Finely grated zest of 1 lemon
- 1tsp vanilla extract
- 1tbsp lemon juice
- 100g (3½oz) icing sugar
- 125g (4oz) blueberries

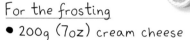

Lemon

Sour cream   Blueberries   Butter

Equipment

Metal spoon

- 23cm (9") springform round cake tin
- Baking paper
- Two large mixing bowls
- Electric or hand whisk
- Metal spoon
- Cooling rack
- Small bowl
- Wooden spoon
- Oven gloves
- Palette knife   ● Sieve

1 Preheat the oven to 180°C (350°F, gas mark 4). Grease a 23cm (9") round springform cake tin and line the base with baking paper to prevent the cake from sticking.

2 Place the butter and caster sugar in a large mixing bowl. Using an electric or hand whisk, cream the butter and sugar together until they are light

3 Whisk in a little of the sour cream until the mixture is smooth. Then whisk in the remaining sour cream, eggs and vanilla extract until thoroughly combined and smooth.

Variation

Fresh raspberries will also work in this recipe. Replace the blueberries in Steps 4 and 6 with the same weight of raspberries.

4 Sift the flour and baking powder over the mixture and gently fold together using a metal spoon. Gently fold in the blueberries, then spoon the mixture into the tin. Level the top.

5 Bake for 45–50 minutes or until the cake feels firm. Leave the cake to cool in the tin for 10 minutes, then tip out onto a cooling rack and peel off the paper. Leave to cool completely.

6 Beat the cream cheese, lemon zest and juice with a wooden spoon in a bowl. Sift over the icing sugar and beat in. Spread the frosting on the cake and decorate with blueberries.

Cake Roll

Deliciously light sponge is combined with fruity jam in this classic cake. The technique can be tricky to master, so you might need to ask an adult to help you.

Variation

For a chocolate cake roll, replace 25g (1oz) of the flour with cocoa powder. This variation is delicious filled with chocolate buttercream icing.

1 Preheat the oven to 200°C (400°F, gas mark 6). Brush the base and sides of a 33cm x 23cm (13" x 9") tin with a little vegetable oil, then line with baking paper. Brush with a little more oil.

2 Whisk the eggs and sugar together in a bowl, using an electric whisk. Whisk for about 10 minutes until the mixture is light and frothy and the whisk leaves a trail when lifted.

Cakes

Ingredients

- 1tbsp vegetable oil
- 3 large eggs
- 125g (4oz) caster sugar, plus extra
- 125g (4oz) self-raising flour

For the filling
- 5tbsp raspberry jam

Equipment

- 33 x 23cm (13 x 9") tin
- Pastry brush
- Baking paper
- Large mixing bowl
- Electric whisk
- Sieve
- Metal spoon
- Oven gloves
- Clean damp tea towel
- Sharp knife
- Palette knife

Sharp knife · *Electric whisk* · *Palette knife* · *Large mixing bowl*

3 Sift the flour into the mixture, carefully folding at the same time with a metal spoon. Pour the mixture into the prepared tin and give it a gentle shake so that the mixture is level.

4 Place the filled tin on the top shelf of the oven. Bake for about 10 minutes or until the sponge is a golden brown and begins to shrink from the edges of the tin.

5 Lay out a damp tea towel on the work surface. Place a piece of baking paper a little bigger than the size of the tin onto the tea towel and sprinkle it with caster sugar.

6 Using oven gloves, tip the warm cake out onto the sugared paper so it is upside down. Take off the gloves and gently loosen the baking paper and peel it off.

7 Trim the edges of the sponge with a sharp knife. Make a score mark 2.5cm (1") from one shorter edge, being careful not to cut right through. This makes the cake easier to roll.

8 Leave the sponge to cool slightly, then spread the jam over it with a palette knife. Roll up the cake firmly from the cut end. Place the cake on a plate seam side down and serve in slices.

Tropical Fruit Cake

This cake is really simple to make. It uses pineapple and mango to add a tropical flavour, but you can use any of your favourite dried fruit.

Variation

This recipe can be made into a traditional fruit cake by replacing the tropical fruit with currants, sultanas, more raisins and glacé cherries.

Ingredients

Raisins

Beaten egg

- 250g (9oz) soft mixed dried tropical fruit e.g. pineapple, mango, papaya, apricots
- 100g (3½oz) raisins
- 1tsp mixed spice

Sugar

- 125g (4oz) butter (diced)
- 125g (4oz) soft brown sugar
- 150ml (¼pt) cold water
- 225g (8oz) self-raising flour
- 1 egg (beaten)

Apricots

Equipment

- 900g (2lb) loaf tin
- Baking paper or loaf tin liner
- Chopping board
- Sharp knife
- Medium saucepan
- Wooden spoon
- Skewer
- Oven gloves

Loaf tin

Chopping board

1 Grease and line the base of a 900g (2lb) loaf tin (or use a loaf tin liner). On a chopping board, carefully cut the tropical fruit into small pieces with a sharp knife.

2 Place the raisins, dried tropical fruit, mixed spice, butter, sugar and water in a medium saucepan. Warm over a low heat until the butter has melted, stirring with a wooden spoon.

3 Bring the butter and fruit mixture to the boil and allow it to simmer for 5 minutes. Then remove the saucepan from the heat and leave the mixture to cool completely.

4 Preheat the oven to 150°C (300°F, gas mark 2). When the mixture is cool, stir in the flour and the egg with the wooden spoon until combined. Then spoon it into the prepared tin.

5 Bake in the centre of the oven for 50–60 minutes, or until a skewer inserted into the middle comes out clean. Leave the cake to cool in the tin. When cool, serve in slices.

Chef's Tip

This cake tastes great served in thin slices, spread with a little butter.

Sticky Date Muffins

These muffins taste light and luscious! The secret to good muffins is to not over-beat the batter otherwise they will be heavy and dense. For the perfect muffins give the mixture a gentle stir with a wooden spoon until the flour just disappears.

Did you know?
Dates are the fruit of the date palm tree, which can grow up to 25 metres (82 feet) tall. Egypt is the world's largest producer

Ingredients

 caster sugar

 egg

- 200g (7oz) white or wholemeal plain flour
- 1 tbsp baking powder
- 125g (4oz) caster sugar
- 1 tsp ground cinnamon
- ½ tsp salt
- 125g (4oz) ready-to-eat dried chopped dates

- 1 tbsp orange juice
- 175ml (6fl oz) milk
- 1 large egg (lightly beaten)
- 140g (5oz) butter

 ground cinnamon

 wholemeal flour

Equipment

 blender

- large muffin tin
- sieve
- large mixing bowl
- wooden spoon
- food processor or blender
- small saucepan
- jug   ● fork
- wire rack
- paper cases

large muffin tin

1 Preheat the oven to 200°C (400°F/gas mark 6). Line the muffin tin with the paper cases. Sift the flour and baking powder into a bowl.

2 Stir the sugar, cinnamon, and salt into the flour and baking powder. Put the dates and orange juice in a blender and whiz until they form a smooth purée.

3 Melt the butter in a saucepan over a low heat. Pour the milk into a jug and add the egg, melted butter, and date purée. Beat together lightly with a fork.

Tasty Twists

Fresh fruit such as blueberries, raspberries, and strawberries make a delicious alternative to the puréed dates. Alternatively, try other dried fruits such as raisins, cherries, apricots, cranberries, or prunes.

Food Facts

Dates are one of the oldest cultivated fruits in the world and have been around since about 6000 BCE. They are soft and tasty and a natural sweetener. Dates are also a good source of iron, fibre, and potassium as well as being low in fat.

dates

4 Pour the date mixture into the flour mixture. Fold the ingredients together gently and evenly with a wooden spoon until the flour is just mixed in.

5 Spoon the mixture into the paper cases until it is almost to the top. Bake for 20 minutes until risen and golden. Transfer the muffins to a wire rack to cool.

Orange and Poppy Seed Muffins

These scrumptious muffins have a zingy fresh orange taste and the poppy seeds add a slight crunch to the texture.

Variation
Add 1tsp ground cinnamon instead of poppy seeds in Step 3 for cinnamon and orange muffins.

Ingredients
- 2 large oranges
- 275g (10oz) self-raising flour
- ½tsp bicarbonate of soda
- ½tsp salt
- 100g (3½oz) caster sugar
- 2tbsp poppy seeds (optional)
- 1 large egg (beaten)
- 90ml (3floz) sunflower oil

Orange icing
- 75g (3oz) icing sugar
- 2 tsp grated orange zest✳
- 2–3tsp orange juice

(✳use the zest from the oranges used in the main recipe)

Equipment
- 2 x 6-hole or 12-hole muffin tin
- Paper muffin cases
- Grater
- Sharp knife
- Juicer
- Measuring jug
- Large mixing bowl
- Sieve
- Metal spoon
- Fork
- Oven gloves
- Cooling rack
- Small mixing bowl

Oven gloves

1 Preheat the oven to 375°F (190°C, gas mark 5). Line a muffin tin (or tins) with 10 paper muffin cases. Finely grate the zest from the oranges with a grater.

2 Cut the oranges in half and squeeze the juice into a jug, removing any pips. You should have about 180ml (6floz) orange juice. Add water to make it up to this amount if necessary.

3 In a large mixing bowl, sift the flour, bicarbonate of soda and salt. Stir in the caster sugar, poppy seeds and 1tbsp of the orange zest. Using a metal spoon, mix together.

4 Add the beaten egg and oil to the orange juice and beat together with a fork. Pour the mixture into the bowl and stir until just combined. Don't worry – the batter will be lumpy!

5 Spoon into the cases and cook in the centre of the oven for 20–25 minutes until well risen and golden. Leave to cool for a few minutes, then transfer to a cooling rack.

6 Sift the icing sugar into a small bowl, then add the orange zest and juice. Stir until you have a smooth icing. Drizzle over the muffins when they have completely cooled.

57

Oat and Honey Muffins

These fluffy light muffins are perfect for breakfast or a mid-morning snack because they are packed with nutritious oats and dried fruit.

Ingredients

Honey

- 250g (9oz) plain flour
- 1tbsp baking powder
- 100g (3½oz) porridge oats
- 125g (4oz) ready-to-eat dried apricots (chopped)
- 50g (2oz) soft light brown sugar
- ½tsp salt
- 2 medium eggs (beaten)
- 175ml (6floz) milk
- 75ml (3floz) sunflower oil
- 5tbsp clear honey

Equipment

- 2 x 6-hole or 12-hole muffin tin
- 10 paper muffin cases
- Large mixing bowl
- Sieve
- Wooden spoon
- Large jug
- Fork
- Oven gloves
- Cooling rack

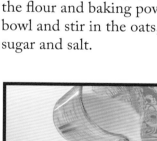
Sieve

1 Preheat the oven to 375°F (190°C, gas mark 5). Line a muffin tin with 10 paper cases. Sift the flour and baking powder into a bowl and stir in the oats, apricots, sugar and salt.

2 Put the flour mixture to one side. In a large jug, beat together the eggs, milk, oil and honey with a fork until thoroughly mixed and frothy.

3 Pour the wet mixture in the jug over the dry ingredients in the bowl. Stir with a wooden spoon until the ingredients are just combined. The batter will be lumpy and quite runny.

4 Divide the mixture between the muffin cases, so they are ⅔ full and cook on the top shelf of the oven for 20–25 minutes. Leave in the tin for a few minutes, then transfer to a cooling rack.

Variation

Don't like apricots?
Just replace them with your
favourite dried fruit, such
as papaya or mango.

Chef's Tip

These muffins taste great
served with yoghurt or fresh
fruit and an extra
drizzle of honey.

Mini Muffins

These bite-sized treats have the delicious combination of tasty banana and melt-in-your-mouth chocolate chips. They are perfect for lunch boxes or for a light snack.

Variation

Try using white chocolate chips or chunks in Step 5 instead of milk chocolate chips. You could also experiment with other flavours of chocolate.

Ingredients

- 280g (10oz) plain flour
- 1tbsp baking powder
- ½tsp salt
- 125g (4oz) caster sugar
- 2 large ripe bananas (peeled and roughly chopped)
- 1 large egg

Milk

Plain flour

- 240ml (8floz) milk
- 85g (3oz) butter (melted)
- 175g (6oz) milk chocolate chips or chunks

Large egg

Butter

Sugar

Bananas

Equipment

- 24-hole mini-muffin tin
- Mini-muffin paper cases (optional)
- Large mixing bowl
- Sieve
- Wooden spoon
- Small mixing bowl
- Fork
- Small hand whisk
- Jug
- Teaspoon ● Oven gloves

Mixing bowl

1 Preheat the oven to 200°C (400°F, gas mark 6). Grease a 24-hole mini-muffin tin with butter (or line it with mini-muffin paper cases) to stop the muffins from sticking.

2 In a large mixing bowl, sift together the flour, baking powder and salt. Stir in the sugar with a wooden spoon until all the ingredients are thoroughly mixed.

3 In a small mixing bowl, mash the two ripe bananas with a fork until nearly smooth but with a few lumps remaining – this will give a nice texture to the muffins.

4 In a jug, whisk together the egg, milk and butter, then pour onto the mashed banana in the bowl. Stir the ingredients together until they are combined thoroughly.

5 Add the egg and banana mixture to the flour mixture. Stir the ingredients together with a wooden spoon to just combine, then fold in the chocolate chips or chunks.

6 Spoon the mixture into the tin and bake for 10–12 minutes. Leave the cakes to cool in the tin then remove them and repeat with the remaining ingredients to make a second batch.

Upside-down Apple Cake

This fruity cake is fun to make and impressive to look at!
Rings look prettier, but slices of apple or pineapple also work.

Chef's Tip
Use a sealed cake tin to prevent the cinnamon butter leaking out over the oven.

1 Preheat the oven to 180°C (350°F, gas mark 4). Grease the base and sides of a 20cm (8") round cake tin, 7.5cm (3") deep. The cake tin should not be a springform or loose-bottomed one.

2 Peel the apples with a peeler, then using a corer remove the cores from the centres. Cut each apple into 5 rings and place in the bottom of the tin, overlapping if necessary.

Ingredients

For the topping
- 2 eating apples
- 50g (2oz) butter (diced)
- 50g (2oz) light muscovado sugar
- 1tsp ground cinnamon (optional)

Apples

Milk

For the cake
- 125g (4oz) butter (softened)
- 125g (4oz) caster sugar
- 2 large eggs
- 125ml (4floz) milk
- ½tsp bicarbonate of soda
- 175g (6oz) self-raising flour

Equipment
- 20cm (8") round cake tin
- Sharp knife • Peeler
- Chopping board • Corer
- Small mixing bowl
- Spoon • Sieve
- Large mixing bowl
- Electric or hand whisk
- Spatula • Oven gloves

Variation
To make a pineapple upside-down cake, replace the apples with canned pineapple rings in natural juice. Drain the rings well on kitchen paper and miss out the cinnamon from the topping mixture.

3 In a small mixing bowl mix together the diced butter, sugar (and cinnamon if you are using it) and sprinkle the mixture over the apple rings in the bottom of the cake tin.

4 Place the butter and sugar in a large bowl. Using an electric or hand whisk beat them together until pale and fluffy. Whisk in the eggs, adding a little flour if the mixture starts to curdle.

5 Whisk in the milk and bicarbonate of soda a little at a time, with some of the flour. Sift over the remaining flour and stir the mixture together until they are just combined.

6 Pour the cake mixture over the apple rings and spread evenly, using a spatula. Bake the cake in the centre of the oven for 30–35 minutes, until golden and firm to the touch.

7 Cool the cake in the tin for 5 minutes, then turn it out. Serve the apple upside-down cake in slices. It can be eaten cold or warm with custard, cream or ice cream.

Fondant Fancies

These gorgeous cakes take a while to prepare
but are well worth the effort.

You can be really creative when you come to decorate these cakes!

Ingredients

Cake:
- 200g (7oz) unsalted butter or margarine (softened)
- 200g (7oz) caster sugar
- grated zest 1 lemon
- 4 medium eggs, beaten
- 200g (7oz) self-raising flour

self-raising flour

Filling and icing:
- 75g (3oz) unsalted butter
- 175g (6oz) icing sugar (sifted)
- 90 to 120ml (6 to 8tbsp) water
- 15ml (1tbsp) milk
- 15ml (1tbsp) apricot jam
- 100g (3½ oz) marzipan
- 1kg (2lb 4oz) icing sugar
- 2-3 drops pink food colouring

lemon

Equipment
- 2 bowls
- 2 spoons
- 20cm (8in) square tin
- baking paper
- electric whisk
- palette knife
- bread knife
- cling film
- rolling pin
- fork

palette knife

1 Preheat the oven to 180ºC, 350ºF, gas mark 4. Grease and line the cake tin. Cream together the butter, sugar and lemon zest.

2 Whisk in the eggs a little at a time, adding a little flour to prevent the mixture curdling. Fold in the rest of the flour. Spoon into the tin and smooth the top.

3 Bake for 20 to 25 minutes. Cool in the tin. Turn out and with a bread knife remove the top layer of the cake, to make it even then cut the cake in half horizontally.

4 Cream together the butter and icing sugar, then add the milk and spread over one half of the cake. Sandwich together. Wrap in cling film and chill for at least 2 hours.

5 Warm the apricot jam and spread over the top. Roll out the marzipan to a 20cm (8in) square and place on top of the cake. Cut the cake into 25 cubes.

6 Mix the fondant icing sugar and water until smooth. Add the pink colouring. Holding over the bowl, drizzle over each cube and decorate as desired. Leave to set.

Biscuits and Cookies

Biscuits and Cookies come in all shapes and sizes. They look and taste yummy and always delight your family and friends at teatime.

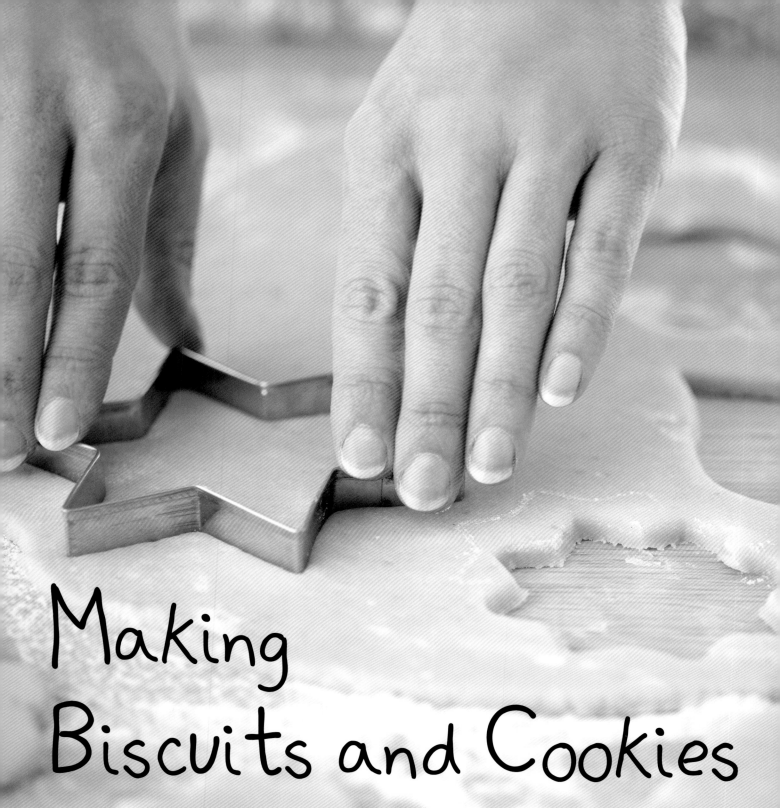

Making Biscuits and Cookies

In this section there are lots of delicious recipes for individual baked treats. Biscuits, cookies and traybakes are quite easy to make and because they often don't need long to cook, they are perfect for a quick baking session.

Mixing

Mixing means putting ingredients together. You can do this by hand, or with a spoon, hand whisk, electric whisk or food processor.

Top Tip

When you are cutting out shapes for biscuits, cut out as many as you can and then gather up the scraps and roll them out again. Repeat until you have used up all the dough and none is wasted.

Rolling and cutting out

When rolling out dough with a rolling pin, make sure the work surface and the rolling pin are sprinkled with flour to prevent the dough from sticking. When cutting out, gently wiggle the cutter from side to side – you will find it lifts out easily.

Top Tip

Always use unsalted butter unless the recipe tells you otherwise. Salted butter burns more easily and is less healthy.

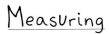

Measuring

Measuring out ingredients is important. The ingredients in these recipes have been carefully calculated so that the finished baked foods turn out just right. The amounts needed are given in metric and imperial measurements. Always stick to one version.

Storage

If you have any leftovers or want to save your creations for later, put them in a sealed, airtight container to keep them fresh.

Toffee Squares

These toffee squares are yummy! For extra stickiness the squares are topped with a caramel toffee sauce. You can buy this in a jar but it's more fun to make your own.

Ingredients

- 150g (5oz) pitted soft dates (roughly chopped)
- 125ml (4floz) cold water
- 1tsp bicarbonate of soda
- 150g (5oz) butter (softened)
- 150g (5oz) light muscovado sugar
- 2 medium eggs (beaten)
- 1tsp vanilla extract
- 175g (6oz) self-raising flour

Toffee topping
- 6tbsp caramel toffee sauce (Dulce de Leche)

Dates

Beaten eggs

Butter

Self-raising flour

Equipment

- 28cm x 18cm (11"x7") tin
- Baking paper
- Small saucepan
- Large mixing bowl
- Electric or hand whisk
- Metal spoon
- Oven gloves
- Cooling rack
- Chopping board
- Sharp knife
- Palette knife

Small saucepan

Chef's Tip
These cakes taste delicious served warm drizzled with caramel sauce and cream or ice cream.

1 Preheat the oven to 180°C (350°F, gas mark 4). Lightly grease a 28cm x 18cm (11" x 7") tin and line the base with baking paper to prevent the cake from sticking.

2 Place the dates in a pan and add the water. Bring to the boil, then remove from the heat and add the bicarbonate of soda – the mixture will fizz! Leave to one side to cool slightly.

3 Place the butter and sugar in a large mixing bowl. Using an electric or hand whisk, beat them together until they are light and fluffy. Whisk in the eggs and vanilla extract.

4 Using a metal spoon fold in the flour, then the date mixture. Pour the mixture into the tin. Place it in the centre of the oven and cook for 25–30 minutes, or until risen.

5 Allow the cake to cool in the tin for 10 minutes, then transfer it to a cooling rack. When cold, cut it into 24 squares, then spread your caramel sauce over the top with a palette knife.

Chef's Tip
To make your own caramel sauce, bring 75g (3oz) butter, 150g (5oz) light brown soft sugar and 150ml (¼pt) single cream to the boil and cook for 3 minutes, until thickened. Allow to cool.

Chocolate Fridge Squares

These crunchy chocolate fruit and nut squares couldn't be easier to make – they don't even need cooking!

Golden syrup

Butter

Apricots

Chocolate

Equipment

- 18cm x 28cm (11" x 7") cake tin
- Baking paper
- Saucepan
- Wooden spoon
- Large mixing bowl
- Blunt knife
- Chopping board

Wooden spoon

Chopping board

Ingredients

- 200g (7oz) 70% cocoa plain chocolate (broken into pieces)
- 100g (3½ oz) butter (diced)
- 4 tbsp golden syrup
- 225g (8oz) digestive biscuits (broken into pieces)
- 125g (4oz) whole shelled pistachios
- 200g (7oz) dried apricots (roughly chopped)
- 100g (3½ oz) dried cranberries or cherries

Chef's Tip

For a citrus twist, add the grated zest of an orange to the chocolate, butter and golden syrup mixture.

1 Line a 18cm x 28cm (11" x 7") tin with baking paper. Place the chocolate, butter and golden syrup in a saucepan over a low heat. Stir occasionally until they are melted and smooth.

2 Place all the remaining ingredients in a large mixing bowl and mix well. Pour over the chocolate mixture and stir until all the ingredients are evenly coated.

Variation
You can replace the dried cranberries or cherries with the same quantity of currants, raisins, glacé cherries or prunes.

3 Tip the mixture into the prepared tin and spread it evenly with the back of a spoon. Chill for at least 2 hours or until firm to the touch.

4 Run a blunt knife around the edge of the tin. Carefully turn out onto a chopping board and remove the baking paper. Cut the fridge cake into squares and serve.

Rocky Road Cookies

These gorgeous cookies are topped with chunky chocolate and melted marshmallows. The chunky and smooth textures are a perfect combination – yum!

Ingredients

- 125g (4oz) butter (softened)
- 125g (4oz) soft brown sugar
- 1 medium egg (beaten)
- 50g (2oz) milk chocolate (chopped)
- 125g (4oz) plain flour
- 1tbsp cocoa powder

Plain flour

Brown sugar

Brown sugar

- ½tsp baking powder
- 50g (2oz) white chocolate (chopped)
- 25g (1oz) mini marshmallows

Equipment

- Two baking sheets
- Baking paper
- Large mixing bowl
- Electric or hand whisk
- Metal spoon
- Oven gloves • Dessert spoon
- Palette knife • Cooling rack

1 Preheat the oven to 180°C (375°F, gas mark 4). Line two baking sheets with baking paper. Use an electric or hand whisk to cream the butter and sugar together in a mixing bowl.

2 Beat in the egg and milk. Then stir in the flour, cocoa powder, baking powder and half the chunks of milk and white chocolate using a metal spoon.

3 Place dessert spoons of the mixture onto the prepared baking sheets, spacing them well apart. Flatten slightly and bake for 5 minutes, until the edges are starting to get firm.

4 Remove the cookies from the oven. Immediately sprinkle them with the marshmallows and remaining chocolate chunks, pressing them down into the cookies.

5 Return the cookies to the oven for a further 5–6 minutes or until slightly soft to the touch. Allow them to cool for 5 minutes, then transfer them to a cooling rack.

Variation

Experiment with different flavoured chocolate chunks. Or try heart-shaped marshmallows for a Valentine's Day treat!

Raisin Biscuits

These simply scrumptious biscuits are sure to become a favourite. They are perfect for an afternoon snack or a light dessert.

Variation
Replace the raisins with currants if you prefer them or spice things up by adding a little cinnamon or mixed spice.

Ingredients

- 125g (4oz) butter (softened)
- 75g (3oz) caster sugar
- Finely grated zest of 1 lemon
- 1 egg (separated)
- 200g (7oz) plain flour (sifted)
- 75g (3oz) raisins
- 2tbsp milk
- 1–2tbsp caster sugar (for sprinkling)

 Lemon

 Baking sheet

Equipment

- Two large baking sheets
- Large mixing bowl
- Electric or hand whisk
- Round-bladed knife
- Rolling pin
- 6cm (2.5") round fluted cutter
- Oven gloves
- Fork
- Pastry brush
- Palette knife
- Cooling rack

 Electric whisk

1 Preheat the oven to 180°C (350°F, gas mark 4). Grease two baking sheets. In a bowl, beat the butter, sugar and lemon zest together using an electric or hand whisk, until they are pale and fluffy.

2 Beat in the egg yolk but keep the egg white to one side. Using a round-bladed knife, gently stir in the sifted flour and raisins. Gradually stir in the milk until the dough comes together.

3 Tip the dough onto a lightly floured surface and knead it gently until it is smooth and supple. Shape the dough into a ball with your hands.

4 Roll the dough out to about 5mm (¼") thick then cut out the biscuits using a 6cm (2.5") round fluted cutter. Place the biscuits on the baking sheets and bake for 8–10 minutes.

5 Using oven gloves, remove the baking sheets from the oven. Lightly whisk the egg white with a fork, then brush it over the biscuits with a pastry brush and sprinkle them with caster sugar.

6 Wearing the oven gloves, return the biscuits to the oven for 3–4 minutes until they turn golden. Once cooked, remove the biscuits from the oven and transfer them to a cooling rack.

Melting Moments

These melt-in-the-mouth biscuits are a chocolate-lover's dream! The creamy filling and crunchy biscuit is a tasty combination.

Chef's Tip
For a perfect professional finish, use a piping bag with a star-shaped nozzle in Step 3. See page 16 and 127 for tips on how to make your own piping bag.

Ingredients

- 175g (6oz) butter (softened)
- 50g (2oz) caster sugar
- 1tsp vanilla extract
- 125g (4oz) plain flour
- 25g (1oz) cornflour
- 25g (1oz) cocoa powder (sifted)

For the filling
- 100g (3½oz) good quality chocolate (broken into pieces)
- 2tbsp double cream

Equipment

- Two large baking sheets
- Baking paper
- Large mixing bowl
- Electric whisk or wooden spoon
- Sieve
- Metal spoon
- Teaspoon
- Oven gloves
- Cooling rack
- Palette knife
- Heatproof bowl
- Small saucepan
- Wooden spoon

Palette knife

Oven gloves

Baking sheet

Sieve

Heatproof bowl

1 Preheat the oven to 180°C (350°F, gas mark 4). Line two baking sheets with baking paper. Place the butter, sugar and vanilla extract in a bowl and beat with a whisk or wooden spoon.

2 Sift the plain flour, cornflour and cocoa powder into the mixing bowl. Using a metal spoon, fold them into the mixture until the ingredients are well combined.

3 Using a teaspoon, spoon 15 x 2.5cm (1") dollops onto each baking sheet so that you have 30 in total. Allow room between each one as they will spread whilst cooking.

4 Bake for 12–15 minutes, or until they are just starting to become dark around the edges. Remove them from the oven and leave to cool slightly before moving to a cooling rack.

5 Place the chocolate and cream in a heatproof bowl over a saucepan of simmering water. Stir them until they have melted. Remove from the heat and leave to cool completely.

6 Spread the filling on the flat side of half of the cooled biscuits with a palette knife and sandwich each one with one of the remaining biscuits.

79

Jam Shapes

These pretty jam-filled biscuits take time to make, but they are definitely worth the effort! The combination of gooey jam and crunchy biscuit is heavenly.

1 Preheat the oven to 170°C (325°F, gas mark 3). Line two baking sheets with baking paper. Process the butter, sugar, vanilla extract and lemon zest in a food processor until smooth.

2 Add the egg, egg yolk and flour to the food processor and process again until the mixture resembles breadcrumbs and is starting to come together in a dough.

3 Transfer the dough to a lightly floured surface and lightly knead until it is smooth. Flatten into a circle, wrap it in cling film and chill for 30 minutes.

Ingredients

- 175g (6oz) butter (softened)
- 175g (6oz) caster sugar
- 1tsp vanilla extract
- 1tsp finely grated lemon zest
- 1 medium egg (beaten)
- 1 egg yolk
- 275g (10oz) plain flour, plus a little extra for rolling out
- 6tbsp raspberry or strawberry jam
- 2tbsp icing sugar (for dusting)

Equipment

- Two large baking sheets
- Baking paper
- Food processor
- Cling film
- Rolling pin
- 6cm (2½") cookie cutter
- 2–3cm (1–1½") cookie cutter
- Oven gloves
- Cooling rack
- Palette knife

Baking sheet

Food processor

Chef's Tip

Use different shaped cutters for different shaped biscuits. Make sure that any cutter that you use has a smaller version to cut the hole out of the middle.

4 On a lightly floured surface, roll the dough out to 3mm (¼") thick. Using a 6cm (2½") cookie cutter, cut out as many biscuits as you can. You should get about 36 in total.

5 Use a 2–3cm (1–1½") cookie cutter to cut out the middle from 18 of the biscuits (you can bake these too if you like). Arrange on the baking sheets and chill for 15 minutes.

6 Bake on the middle shelf of the oven (in batches, if necessary) for about 10–12 minutes or until golden. Cool on the baking sheets for 1 minute, then transfer them to a cooling rack.

7 When completely cool, spread the whole biscuits with jam. Then dust icing sugar on the biscuits with holes in. Press one sugar-dusted biscuit onto each jam-covered one and serve.

Variation

You can use any flavour of jam you prefer instead of raspberry or strawberry. Try apricot or blackcurrant jam.

Orange and Seed Cookies

These oaty cookies are flavoured with tangy orange.
The sunflower seeds are a great source of vitamins
and minerals, as well as adding an extra crunch!

Chef's Tip
To make smaller cookies,
place heaped teaspoons instead
of dessert spoons of the
mixture on the trays and
bake for 7–9 minutes.

Ingredients

- 125g (4oz) porridge oats
- 75g (3oz) sunflower seeds
- 150g (5oz) self-raising flour
- 150g (5oz) butter (diced)
- Finely grated zest of 1 orange
- 2tbsp orange juice
- 150g (5oz) soft light brown sugar
- 2tbsp golden syrup

Equipment

- Three large baking trays
- Baking paper
- Large mixing bowl
- Wooden spoon
- Medium saucepan
- Dessert spoon
- Oven gloves
- Cooling rack
- Palette knife

Oven gloves

Saucepan

Wooden spoon

Mixing bowl

1 Preheat the oven to 180°C (350°F, gas mark 4). Line three large baking trays with baking paper to prevent the cookies from sticking to them.

2 Place the oats, sunflower seeds and flour in a large mixing bowl. Stir the mixture with a wooden spoon until completely mixed together. Put the bowl to one side.

3 Place the butter, orange zest, juice, sugar and golden syrup in a medium saucepan. Heat the mixture over a low heat whilst stirring, until the butter and sugar have melted.

4 Carefully pour the butter mixture over the ingredients in the large mixing bowl and mix them together with the wooden spoon until thoroughly combined.

5 Place heaped dessert spoons of the mixture onto each tray. Leave a generous space between each biscuit, as they will spread. Bake for 8–10 minutes, until the cookies are golden.

6 Leave the cookies to cool on the tray for a few minutes, then transfer them to a cooling rack with a palette knife, to become crisp. They will keep in an airtight container for 2–3 days.

Chocolate and Cranberry Cookies

The perfect combination of bitter cranberries and sweet white chocolate makes these cookies melt in your mouth!

Chef's Tip
Eat these moreish cookies while they are still warm – as the chocolate will be gooey. Delicious!

Ingredients

- 125g (4oz) butter (softened)
- 125g (4oz) soft light brown sugar
- 1 medium egg (beaten)
- 1tbsp milk
- 150g (5oz) plain flour
- ½tsp baking powder
- 50g (2oz) white chocolate (finely grated)
- 100g (3½oz) white chocolate chips
- 50g (2oz) dried cranberries

Butter

Brown sugar

Equipment

- Two baking sheets
- Baking paper
- Large mixing bowl
- Electric or hand whisk
- Dessert spoon
- Oven gloves
- Cooling rack
- Flipper

Electric whisk

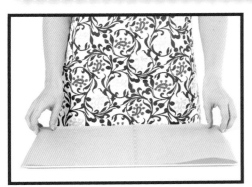

1 Preheat the oven to 180°C (375°F, gas mark 4). Line two baking sheets with baking paper to prevent the cookies from sticking while they are baking.

2 Cream the butter and sugar together in a large bowl until they are pale and creamy. (You can use a hand or electric whisk.) Then beat in the egg and milk with the whisk.

3 Add the flour, baking powder, grated chocolate, chocolate chips and cranberries to the mixture. Using a dessert spoon, stir until they are thoroughly mixed together.

4 Place dessert spoonfuls of the cookie mixture onto the prepared baking sheets. Leave space between the spoonfuls so the cookies do not merge together as they cook.

5 Bake for 12–15 minutes, until lightly golden and slightly soft to the touch. Allow to cool on the sheet for 5 minutes, then transfer to a cooling rack to cool completely.

Variation

Milk or plain chocolate would also taste great in these cookies. If you prefer other dried fruits such as strawberries or blueberries, use them instead of cranberries.

Star Biscuits

These biscuits make great gifts for your friends and family. You can use different shaped cutters for different themes, such as Christmas, Halloween or Valentine's Day.

Chef's Tip
You can hang these biscuits as pretty decorations. Use a skewer to make the hole and thread them with ribbon.

Ingredients

- 200g (7oz) plain flour
- 125g (4oz) butter (diced)
- 100g (3½oz) caster sugar
- 1tsp ground cinnamon
- Finely grated zest of 1 orange
- 1 medium egg, lightly beaten
- 2tbsp golden syrup

To decorate: ribbon, writing icing, edible silver balls or hundreds and thousands

Equipment

- Two large baking sheets
- Baking paper
- Food processor
- Small bowl
- Fork
- Rolling pin
- Star shape cutter
- Bamboo skewer
- Oven gloves
- Cooling rack

Small bowl

Oven gloves

Food processor

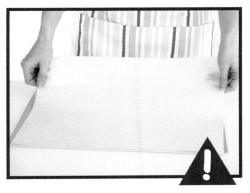

1 Preheat the oven to 180°C (350°F, gas mark 4). Line two large baking sheets with baking paper. Pulse the flour and butter in a food processor, until the mixture resembles fine breadcrumbs.

2 Add the sugar, cinnamon and orange zest and pulse again. In a small bowl, beat together the egg and golden syrup with a fork then add this to the breadcrumb mixture.

3 Process the mixture in the food processor until it comes together in a ball. Lift the ball of dough out, wrap it in cling film and chill for 10 minutes in the fridge.

4 Roll out the chilled dough on a lightly floured surface, to 4–5mm (¼") thickness. Cut into stars using a shaped cutter. Re-roll and cut out more stars until you use up all the dough.

5 Place the stars slightly apart on the baking sheets and cook for 10–12 minutes. Allow to cool for 2 minutes and if they are decorations, poke a hole in the top of each using the skewer.

6 Transfer the stars to a cooling rack. When they are cool, decorate them as desired. Thread the holes with ribbon and tie the ends together if you are making them as decorations.

Flapjacks

Tasty crumbly oats mixed with sticky golden syrup and crunchy corn flakes make these flapjacks completely irresistible. Oats release energy slowly so you won't feel hungry again for a while.

Ingredients

- 175g (6oz) butter (diced)
- 175g (6oz) soft light brown sugar
- 4tbsp golden syrup
- 350g (12oz) whole jumbo porridge oats
- 50g (2oz) corn flakes

Equipment

- Large saucepan
- Wooden spoon
- 28cm × 18cm (11" × 7") tin
- Oven gloves
- Sharp knife

Sharp knife

Large saucepan

Chef's Tip

Don't be tempted to take the flapjacks out of the tin until they are completely cooled, or they will break up.

Chef's Tip

Cut the flapjacks into bars while they are still slightly warm otherwise they will be too hard to cut.

1 Preheat the oven to 180°C (350°F, gas mark 4). In a saucepan, gently melt the butter, sugar and golden syrup over a low heat, stirring with a wooden spoon until the sugar has dissolved.

2 Remove the saucepan from the heat and gently stir in the porridge oats and the corn flakes with the wooden spoon, until the mixture is thoroughly combined and sticky.

3 Tip the mixture into a 28cm x 18cm (11"x 7") tin and spread it into the corners. Gently press down with the back of the wooden spoon to make the top flat and even.

4 Bake the mixture for 25 minutes, or until golden and firm. Allow to cool for 10 minutes then cut it into bars. Leave to cool completely before lifting the bars out of the tin.

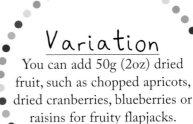

Variation

You can add 50g (2oz) dried fruit, such as chopped apricots, dried cranberries, blueberries or raisins for fruity flapjacks.

Ginger and Pumpkin Slices

This sticky pumpkin and ginger cake is wonderfully dark and moist. It tastes even better the day after baking – if you can resist eating it for that long!

Ingredients

Plain flour

Golden syrup

Sugar

Eggs

Butter

- 125g (4oz) butter
- 75g (3oz) dark muscovado sugar
- 150g (5oz) golden syrup
- 150g (5oz) black treacle
- 250g (9oz) pumpkin (grated)
- 300g (11oz) plain flour
- 1tsp bicarbonate of soda
- 2tsp ground ginger
- Two medium eggs (beaten)

Equipment

- 23cm (9") square cake tin
- Baking paper
- Medium saucepan
- Wooden spoon
- Large mixing bowl
- Oven gloves
- Chopping board
- Sharp knife

Chopping board

Square cake tin

Variation
If pumpkins are not in season, use grated butternut squash instead. They have a similar flavour as they are both part of the squash family of vegetables.

1 Grease the base of a 23cm (9") square cake tin with a bit of butter on some baking paper and line it with baking paper. Preheat the oven to 180°C (350°F, gas mark 4).

2 Place the butter, sugar, golden syrup and treacle in a medium pan and heat gently until the sugar has dissolved and the butter has melted. Remove it from the heat and allow to cool.

Chef's Tip
Instead of lime zest and juice, add 2tsp vanilla extract in Step 2. Stir a little vanilla extract and water in Step 5 instead of lime zest and juice.

3 In a large mixing bowl, add the grated pumpkin or butternut squash, plain flour, bicarbonate of soda and ginger. Mix thoroughly with a wooden spoon.

4 Stir in the treacle mixture and beaten eggs until combined, then pour into the greased and lined tin. Bake in the middle of the oven for 35–40 minutes, or until firm.

5 Allow the cake to cool in the tin. Once cool, carefully tip out onto a chopping board. Peel off the paper from the back and cut the cake into rectangles with a sharp knife.

Coconut Biscuits

Give oat biscuits a tasty tropical twist with creamy coconut. The bicarbonate of soda gives the biscuits a great crunchy texture.

Ingredients

- 75g (3oz) desiccated coconut
- 100g (3½oz) plain flour
- 100g (3½oz) caster sugar
- 100g (3½oz) porridge oats
- 100g (3½oz) butter (diced)
- 1tbsp golden syrup
- 1tsp bicarbonate of soda
- 2tbsp hot water

Golden syrup

Plain flour

Equipment

- Two baking trays
- Baking paper
- Large mixing bowl
- Wooden spoon
- Medium saucepan
- Dessert spoon
- Oven gloves
- Palette knife
- Cooling rack

Mixing bowl

Oven gloves

Saucepan

Chef's Tip
A good way to measure out golden syrup is to lightly grease the tablespoon with a little oil. You'll find the golden syrup will just run off the spoon into the pan.

Chef's Tip
These biscuits will store for up to a week in an airtight container.

1 Preheat the oven to 180°C (350°F, gas mark 4). Line two baking trays with baking paper. Place the coconut, flour, sugar and oats in a mixing bowl and mix together with a wooden spoon.

2 Place the butter and golden syrup in a medium saucepan and heat over a low heat until melted. Stir the mixture with a wooden spoon to mix thoroughly.

3 Mix the bicarbonate of soda with the hot water. Add it to the butter mixture in the saucepan. The bicarbonate will make the butter and golden syrup mixture fizz. Stir well.

4 Pour the butter mixture into the large mixing bowl and mix well. Spoon the mixture onto the baking trays with a dessert spoon, leaving room between each one for the biscuits to spread.

5 Bake the biscuits for 8–10 minutes on the top shelf of the oven until golden. Allow the biscuits to cool on the tray for five minutes, then transfer to a cooling rack to cool completely.

Chocolate Fudge Brownies

These delicious brownies are perfect – crisp on the outside and fudgy on the inside. Be careful not to overcook them as they should be gooey in the centre.

Chef's Tip
These brownies are very rich so you only need to serve them in small squares.

Variation
For nutty brownies, add 150g (5oz) chopped hazelnuts, walnuts, brazil or pecans. In Step 4, for double chocolate brownies, stir in 150g (5oz) white or milk chocolate chips or buttons.

Ingredients

- 250g (9oz) butter
- 275g (10oz) 70% cocoa dark chocolate (broken into pieces)
- 275g (10oz) caster sugar
- Three large eggs
- 1tsp vanilla extract
- 225g (8oz) plain flour
- ½tsp salt

Equipment

Square cake tin

Electric whisk

Saucepan

Wooden spoon

Mixing bowl

- 23cm (9") square cake tin
- Baking paper
- Medium saucepan
- Wooden spoon
- Large mixing bowl
- Electric or hand whisk
- Metal spoon
- Oven gloves
- Cooling rack
- Sharp knife

1 Preheat the oven to 180°C (350°F, gas mark 4). Grease and line the base of a 23cm (9") square cake tin with baking paper to prevent the brownies from sticking.

2 Melt the butter and chocolate in a medium saucepan over a low heat, stirring occasionally with a wooden spoon. Remove the saucepan from the heat and allow to cool slightly.

3 In a large mixing bowl beat together the sugar, eggs and vanilla extract using an electric or hand whisk. Keep whisking until the mixture is pale and fluffy.

4 Whisk the chocolate mixture into the egg mixture until thoroughly combined, using the electric or hand whisk. Then stir in the flour and salt with a metal spoon.

5 Pour the mixture into the prepared tin and cook for 20–25 minutes in the middle of the oven, until the brownies are just set. The centre should be slightly gooey.

6 Leave the cake to cool for 10 minutes in the tin. Tip it onto a cooling rack. When it is completely cold, remove the baking paper and cut the brownies into squares.

Gingerbread

Gingerbread tastes great and smells wonderful as it bakes. This recipe can be used for regular shaped biscuits, pretty tree decorations or gingerbread people.

Ingredients

- 350g (12oz) plain flour
- 2tsp ground ginger
- 1tsp bicarbonate of soda
- 125g (4oz) butter (diced)
- 150g (5oz) soft dark brown sugar
- 4tbsp golden syrup
- 1 medium egg (beaten)
- Sweets, currants and icing for decoration

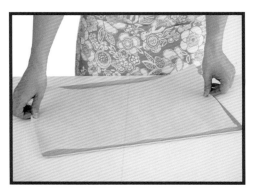
Brown sugar

Equipment

- Two large baking trays
- Baking paper
- Large mixing bowl
- Wooden spoon
- Rolling pin
- Cutters of your choice
- Oven gloves

Oven gloves
Mixing bowl

Chef's Tip

These biscuits can be stored in an airtight container for two days. To use as decorations, punch a hole through the biscuit with a skewer once cooked and thread a ribbon through.

1 Preheat the oven to 180°C (350°F, gas mark 4). Line two large baking trays with baking paper. If you only have one tray, you will need to cook the biscuits in two batches.

2 Place the flour, ginger and bicarbonate of soda in a large bowl. Stir the ingredients together with a wooden spoon until they are thoroughly mixed.

3 Rub the butter into the mixture using your fingertips. Continue rubbing in the butter until the mixture resembles fine breadcrumbs. Stir in the sugar.

4 Stir in the golden syrup and egg, until the mixture starts to come together in a dough. Tip the dough mixture onto a lightly floured surface and knead it until smooth.

5 Roll out the dough on a lightly floured surface to a thickness of 5mm (¼"), then using your cutters, cut out the shapes. Re-roll the leftover dough and cut out more biscuits.

6 Place the biscuits on the baking trays and cook for 9–10 minutes or until golden. Allow the biscuits to cool on the trays. Decorate with sweets, currants and icing.

Desserts

These desserts can be enjoyed at any time, and not just after a meal. Most can be made even more luscious by topping with cream or ice-cream.

Making Pastry

Pastry is made using flour, fat and water and there are many different types. Puff, shortcrust and filo pastry can be bought fresh or frozen in the shops, and work well in the following recipes. If you have time, you can make your own shortcrust pastry using the simple recipe opposite.

Different types of pastry

Choux pastry is used for profiterôles and éclairs. Shortcrust pastry is used for making pies and tarts and can be sweet or savoury. Puff pastry is used for pies and baked slices. Filo is lots of thin layers of pastry and is used for sweet and savoury pies and tarts.

Top Tip
When rolling out pastry, use a cool surface and dust the surface and rolling pin with a little flour. Glazing pastry with beaten egg or milk will give it an appetising sheen.

How to make shortcrust pastry

1. In a bowl, sift 225g (8oz) plain flour with a pinch of salt. Add 125g (4oz) diced butter and rub this into the flour using your fingertips.

2. Stir in 3–4tbsp of cold water with a round-bladed knife until the mixture begins to stick together and form a dough.

3. Knead the dough lightly on a floured work surface until smooth. Wrap it in cling film and chill it for 30 minutes before you use it.

Top Tip
Pastry will be much easier to handle if you make sure your hands are cold when making it. Hot hands will make the butter in the pastry melt.

Baking blind

Baking blind is when you bake a pastry case with baking beans inside it instead of the filling. This seals the pastry and stops it from rising. You then bake it again with the filling inside. If you don't have baking beans, you can use scrunched up aluminium foil.

Oaty Crumble

Fruit crumble is one of the great British puddings. It is easy to make but tastes so good it's very difficult to resist! Give this traditional dish a healthy twist by adding oats and seeds to the topping.

Tasty Twists

Try different varieties of fruit. Seasonal fruit tends to have the best flavour so in the summer months you could try nectarines, peaches, plums, or rhubarb, and in late summer/early autumn try apples, blackberries, or pears.

Ingredients

- 4 dessert apples
- 200g (7oz) blueberries, defrosted if frozen
- 4 tbsp fresh apple juice
- 1 tbsp light muscovado sugar

Topping:

- 75g (3oz) plain white flour
- 75g (3oz) wholemeal flour
- 75g (3oz) unsalted butter (cut into small pieces)
- 75g (3oz) light muscovado sugar
- 3 tbsp sunflower seeds
- 1 tbsp sesame seeds
- 3 tbsp rolled oats

sunflower seeds

muscovado sugar

Equipment

- large mixing bowl
- small sharp knife
- chopping board
- 900ml (2 pint) ovenproof dish
- small jug

sharp knife

chopping board

mixing bowl

1 Preheat the oven to 180°C (350°F/gas mark 4). Put the plain white flour and wholemeal flour into a large mixing bowl and stir together with a spoon.

2 Add the butter. Rub the butter and flour together with your fingertips until they look like coarse breadcrumbs. Stir in the sugar, seeds, and oats.

3 Remove the skin from the apples and cut them into quarters. Then carefully remove the core and slice the fruit into bite-sized pieces.

You can leave the skin on the apples, if you like – it is very good fo you.

4 Put the pieces of apple into an ovenproof dish. Add the blueberries and pour over the apple juice. Sprinkle the sugar evenly over the top.

5 Spoon over the topping in an even layer then put the dish in the oven. Cook for 35 minutes until the top is crisp and beginning to brown.

Food Facts

For such a small fruit, blueberries pack a powerful health punch. According to recent research, they beat 40 other fruit and vegetables in helping to prevent certain diseases! They provide a high concentration of antioxidants which means they may help to prevent cancer and heart disease. What's more they may help to fight infections, boost memory and be anti-ageing.

blueberries

Fruit Bread Pudding

This is a quick version of the classic British dessert, summer pudding, which is usually made in a bowl and left overnight to allow the fruit juices to soak into the bread.

Did you know?
The word "companion" comes from the Latin words "com" meaning "with" and "panis" meaning "bread" so it originally meant one with whom bread is shared.

Ingredients

stale wholemeal bread

- 8 slices wholemeal bread (preferably slightly stale)
- 600g (1lb 5oz) mixed fresh or frozen berries such as strawberries, blackberries, blackcurrants, and raspberries

blackberries

- 125ml (4fl oz) water
- 100g (3½ oz) caster sugar

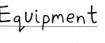
medium saucepan

strawberries

Equipment

sieve

- chopping board
- medium saucepan
- large pastry cutter or scissors
- bowl
- wooden spoon
- sieve
- large shallow dish
- tablespoon
- spatula or fish slice

wooden spoon

1 Cut the bread into your chosen shape using scissors or a large pastry cutter. (Use as much of the bread as possible to avoid waste.)

2 Put all but a handful of the berries, the water, and about two-thirds of the sugar into a saucepan. Stir and then bring to the boil. Reduce the heat.

Food Facts

Bread is a staple food of many European, Middle Eastern, and Indian cultures and is prepared by baking, steaming, or frying dough. There are more than 200 different types of bread but for the healthiest diet, you should try and eat wholegrain varieties which contain more fibre and B vitamins.

bread

3 Simmer the berries gently for about 7 minutes or until the fruit is soft and very juicy. Taste and add the remaining sugar if the fruit is too sharp.

4 Strain the juice from the fruit into a bowl. Press the fruit through a sieve into another bowl to make a purée. Throw away the seeds.

Tasty Twists

This delicious fruit purée would also taste great spooned over pancakes, yoghurt ice cream, or natural yoghurt.

5 Place 4 bread shapes in a large shallow dish and spoon over the fruit purée until the bread is completely covered with the fruit.

6 Add a second piece of bread on top of the first. Spoon over the remaining purée and the berry juice. Gently press the bread with the back of a spoon.

7 Leave for at least 30 minutes to allow the bread to soak up the juice. Carefully lift out of the dish and decorate with the leftover berries and a little juice.

Baked Raspberry Cheesecake

This baked cheesecake is so simple to make. You could replace the raspberries with blueberries if you prefer. Serve at a party for your friends or family.

Variation
Replace the digestive biscuits with chocolate chip cookies. Delicious!

Ingredients

- 200g (7oz) digestive biscuits
- 50g (2oz) butter
- 600g (1lb 4oz) cream cheese
- 142ml pot sour cream
- 25g (1oz) cornflour
- 75g (3oz) icing sugar (sifted)
- 3 medium eggs
- 1tsp vanilla extract

- 225g (8oz) fresh raspberries

Raspberries

To serve
- Fresh raspberries
- Icing sugar (for dusting)

Equipment

- Food bag
- Rolling pin or food processor

Chopping board

- Chopping board
- Wooden spoon
- Saucepan
- 20cm (8") springform round cake tin
- Large mixing bowl
- Electric or hand whisk
- Metal spoon
- Baking tray
- Oven gloves

Saucepan

1 Preheat oven to 170°C (325°F, gas mark 3). Place the biscuits in a food bag and crush them with a rolling pin. (You could also do this with a food processor.).

2 Melt the butter in a saucepan and stir in the crushed biscuits. Press the biscuit mixture into the base of the tin with the back of a spoon. Chill in the fridge for 15 minutes.

3 Place the cream cheese and sour cream in a large mixing bowl. Using an electric or hand whisk, beat the mixture until smooth. Then beat in the cornflour and icing sugar.

4 Add the eggs and vanilla extract to the bowl and whisk until smooth. Using a metal spoon, carefully stir in the raspberries. Pour this mixture over the biscuit base.

5 Place the cake on a baking tray and bake for 35–40 minutes in the middle of the oven until just set. Leave it to cool, then chill the cake in the fridge for 2–3 hours or overnight.

6 Carefully remove the cake from the springform tin and decorate with the fresh raspberries. Dust the cheesecake with icing sugar, and serve it in slices.

Raspberry Cheesecake

This fruity cheesecake is so simple to make. The jelly adds flavour and also sets the cheesecake.

Light, creamy, and delicious, this cheesecake is heavenly to eat.

Ingredients

raspberries

- 75g (3oz) unsalted butter
- 150g (5½ oz) digestive biscuits
- 135g (5oz) pack of raspberry flavour jelly
- 200ml (7floz) evaporated milk, chilled
- 200g (7oz) soft cream cheese

- 100g (3½ oz) raspberries
- a few raspberries for decoration

milk

Equipment

rolling pin

- 20cm (8in) round loose-bottomed sandwich tin
- baking paper
- food bag
- rolling pin
- saucepan
- 3 metal spoons
- heatproof jug
- large bowl
- electric whisk

heatproof jug

1 Line the base of a 20cm (8") round loose-bottomed sandwich tin with baking paper.

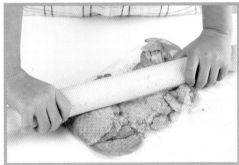

2 Place the biscuits in a food bag and crush with a rolling pin (or you can do this in a food processor).

3 Melt the butter in a saucepan and stir in the crushed biscuits. Press into the tin and chill.

4 Break the jelly into pieces. Then, in a heatproof jug, put the jelly in 100ml (3½floz) boiling water, stir until dissolved.

5 In a large bowl, whisk the milk until light and fluffy and doubled in volume. Whisk in the cream cheese, until the mixture is smooth. Whisk in the jelly.

6 Roughly chop the raspberries and stir into the mixture. Pour over the biscuit base and leave to chill for 2 hours. Serve decorated with extra raspberries.

Strawberry Meringues

These delicious pretty meringues are crisp
on the outside and soft in the middle.
Fill with lightly whipped cream
and sliced strawberries.

Helpful Hints

You can make vanilla sugar by
leaving a vanilla pod in a
jar of sugar.

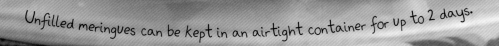

Unfilled meringues can be kept in an airtight container for up to 2 days.

Ingredients

eggs

- 2 large egg whites
- 100g (3½ oz) caster sugar
- 150ml (¼pt) double cream
- 15ml (1tbsp) vanilla sugar
- 12 small strawberries (sliced)

caster sugar

strawberries

Equipment

large mixing bowl

- 2 large baking sheets
- baking paper
- large mixing bowl
- electric whisk
- tablespoon
- teaspoon

baking sheet

1 Preheat the oven to 110°C, 225°F, gas mark ¼. Lightly grease 2 large baking sheets and line with baking paper.

2 Place the egg whites into a large, spotlessly clean mixing bowl and whisk them until they form stiff peaks.

3 Add the sugar a tablespoon at a time, whisking well after each addition, until the mixture is smooth, thick and glossy.

4 Place heaped teaspoons of the mixture, spaced a little apart, onto the prepared baking sheets, until you have 30 meringues. Flatten slightly.

5 Bake in a preheated oven for one hour, or until they peel away from the baking paper. Leave to cool. Whisk the vanilla sugar into the cream until thick.

6 Spread some cream on the flat side of a meringue, put some strawberries on top, spread some cream on another meringue and sandwich together.

Lemon Meringue

This family favourite has crunchy pastry layered with a tangy lemon filling and a soft meringue topping. It's a taste sensation!

1 Preheat the oven to 190°C (375°F, gas mark 5). Roll out the pastry with a rolling pin on a lightly floured surface to about 25cm (10"). Line the flan tin with the pastry and chill for 15 minutes.

2 Prick the pastry case base with a fork, line with baking paper and fill with baking beans or scrunched aluminium foil. Place on a baking tray and bake for 15 minutes.

3 Remove the paper and beans from the pastry case and return to the oven for a further 5 minutes until golden. Then reduce the oven to 150°C (300°F, gas mark 2).

Ingredients

- 175g (6oz) ready-prepared shortcrust pastry

For the filling
- 3tbsp cornflour
- 150ml (¼pt) cold water
- 2 large lemons
- 75g (3oz) caster sugar
- 25g (1oz) butter

- 2 large egg yolks

For the topping
- 2 large egg whites
- 100g (3½oz) • caster sugar

Equipment

- Rolling pin
- 19cm (7½") loose-bottomed round fluted tin

- Fork • Baking paper
- Baking beans or aluminium foil
- Baking tray
- Oven gloves • Tablespoon
- Medium saucepan
- Grater • Sharp knife
- Chopping board
- Jug • Wooden spoon
- Large mixing bowl
- Electric or hand whisk

4 Mix the cornflour and water together in the saucepan. Grate the zest from the lemons, then cut them in half and squeeze the juice into a jug, until you have 150ml (¼pt).

5 Add the lemon zest and juice to the saucepan, then slowly bring to the boil, stirring continuously with a wooden spoon. Simmer, still stirring, until the mixture thickens.

6 Remove the saucepan from the heat and stir in the sugar and butter. Let the mixture cool slightly, then beat in the egg yolks. Pour the mixture into the pastry case.

7 In a clean mixing bowl, whisk the egg whites with an electric or hand whisk until they form stiff peaks. Then whisk in the sugar 1tbsp at a time, until the mixture is thick and glossy.

8 Spoon the meringue mixture over the lemon mixture, leaving the rim of the pastry uncovered. Make peaks in the meringue with the back of the spoon, if you like.

9 Place the pie on the top shelf of the oven and bake for 30–35 minutes, or until the meringue is crisp and golden. Serve cold or warm with cream or ice cream.

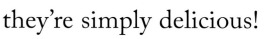

Chocolate Profiteroles

You won't be able to resist these light and fluffy profiterôles. Topped with warm chocolate sauce, they're simply delicious!

1 Preheat the oven to 200°C (400°F, gas mark 6). Grease a baking sheet and sprinkle it with a little cold water. (This will generate steam in the oven and help the choux pastry to rise.)

2 Place the butter and cold water in a medium saucepan and heat gently until the butter has melted. Then turn up the heat and bring them quickly to the boil.

3 Remove the saucepan from the heat and add all the flour at once. Then beat the melted butter and flour together with a wooden spoon until the mixture comes together.

Ingredients

Choux pastry
- 150ml (¼pt) cold water
- 50g (2oz) butter (diced)
- 75g (3oz) plain flour (sifted)
- 2 medium eggs (beaten)

Filling
- ½tsp vanilla extract
- 300ml (½pt) double cream

Chocolate sauce
- 125g (4oz) plain chocolate (broken into small pieces)
- 25g (1oz) butter
- 2tbsp golden syrup

Equipment
- Baking sheet
- Two medium saucepans

Knife

- Wooden spoon
- Dessert spoon
- Oven gloves
- Knife
- Electric or hand whisk
- Large mixing bowl
- Teaspoon
- Heatproof bowl

Mixing bowl

4 Allow the mixture to cool for a couple of minutes. Then beat in the eggs with an electric whisk or wooden spoon, a little at a time, until the mixture becomes smooth and shiny.

5 Use a dessert spoon to place 12 golf ball-sized balls of the pastry on to the baking sheet. Bake the profiteroles at the top of the oven for 20–25 minutes.

6 Using oven gloves, take the cooked profiteroles out of the oven. Make a slit in the side of each with a knife to let the steam out, taking care not to burn your fingers. Allow to cool.

7 Add the vanilla extract and the cream to a large bowl. Whip them to form soft peaks using the electric or hand whisk. Then use the teaspoon to spoon the cream into the buns.

8 Place the chocolate, butter and golden syrup into a heatproof bowl. Place the bowl over a saucepan of simmering water and gently melt the contents. Stir well.

9 Carefully spoon the chocolate sauce over the profiteroles with a dessert spoon. Then serve immediately with any remaining sauce.

Cherry and Berry Pie

This pie is really easy to make – you simply scrunch up ready-prepared puff pastry and fill with your favourite berry fruits! You can serve it with a scoop of vanilla ice cream or cream.

Ingredients

- 500g (1lb 2oz) ready-prepared puff pastry
- 1 egg (beaten)
- 2tbsp semolina
- 650g (1lb 6oz) mixed berries e.g. stoned cherries, blueberries, raspberries, red and blackcurrants
- 2tbsp caster sugar
- Icing sugar (for dusting)

Equipment

- Rolling pin
- 30cm (12") plate
- Sharp knife
- Baking sheet
- Pastry brush
- Teaspoon
- Large mixing bowl
- Large metal spoon
- Oven gloves

Mixing bowl

Large metal spoon

Oven gloves

Chef's Tip

You can use defrosted frozen berries or any drained tinned fruit if fresh berries are not in season.

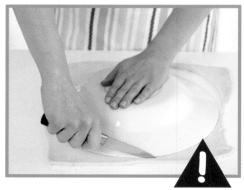

1 Preheat the oven to 200°C (400°F, gas mark 6). Roll out the pastry on a lightly floured surface. Cut around a 30cm (12") plate with a sharp knife to make a circle.

2 Place the pastry circle on a baking sheet. Use a pastry brush to spread the beaten egg on the pastry, then sprinkle over 1tbsp of the semolina with a teaspoon.

3 In a large mixing bowl, place the mixed berries, remaining semolina and 1tbsp caster sugar. Use a large metal spoon to gently mix together, taking care not to crush the berries.

4 Pile the fruit in the centre of the pastry, away from the edge. Scrunch up the edges of the pastry, bringing them towards the centre, but leaving the middle exposed.

5 Brush the scrunched pastry edges with more beaten egg and sprinkle the pastry with the remaining sugar. Chill for 30 minutes in the fridge.

6 Bake the pie at the top of the oven for 30 minutes until golden. If the pastry starts to become too brown, cover the pie with foil. Dust with icing sugar and serve in slices.

Chocolate Tart

This is perfect for chocoholics! This chocolate tart has a tangy orange pastry base. It can be served warm or cold with a dollop of ice cream or cream.

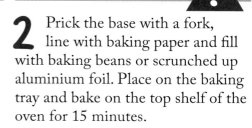

Variation
Any flavour of jam works well spread on the pastry base instead of orange marmalade in Step 3.

1 Preheat the oven to 190°C (375°F, gas mark 5). Using a rolling pin, roll out the pastry on a lightly floured surface and use it to line the flan tin. Chill for 15 minutes.

2 Prick the base with a fork, line with baking paper and fill with baking beans or scrunched up aluminium foil. Place on the baking tray and bake on the top shelf of the oven for 15 minutes.

Ingredients

- 350g (12oz) ready-prepared shortcrust pastry
- 4tbsp orange marmalade
- 200g (7oz) milk chocolate (broken into pieces)
- 2 large eggs (beaten)
- 50g (2oz) caster sugar
- 150ml (¼pt) double cream
- Cocoa powder (for dusting)

Equipment

- Rolling pin
- 23cm (9") loose bottomed flan tin
- Fork
- Baking paper
- Baking beans or aluminium foil

Electric whisk

Saucepan

- Baking tray
- Metal spoon
- Heatproof bowl
- Small saucepan
- Large mixing bowl
- Electric or hand whisk
- Wooden spoon
- Oven gloves

Wooden spoon

Chef's Tip

Placing the tin on a baking tray will help to make the pastry base crisp.

3 Remove the paper and beans from the case and return it to the oven for a further 5 minutes, until golden. Whilst the pastry is still warm, spread the base with the marmalade.

4 Reduce the oven temperature to 160°C (325°F, gas mark 3). Melt the chocolate in a heatproof bowl, over a saucepan of simmering water, whilst stirring. Allow to cool slightly.

5 In a large mixing bowl, place the eggs and sugar and whisk with an electric or hand whisk until pale and fluffy. Whisk in the chocolate until thoroughly combined.

6 Stir in the cream with a wooden spoon. Pour the mixture into the tart case. Bake for about 25–30 minutes on the top shelf of the oven until the tart has just started to set.

7 Remove the tart from the oven. It will continue to set as it cools. Dust with cocoa powder. Serve in slices with a scoop of vanilla ice cream, pouring cream or crème fraîche.

Banoffee Pie

This divinely decadent caramel and banana pie is definitely for those with a sweet tooth!

Chef's Tip
For a really speedy banoffee pie, use a can of shop-bought toffee sauce.

Ingredients

For the base
- 250g (9oz) digestive biscuits
- 125g (4oz) butter

For the filling
- 125g (4oz) butter (diced)
- 125g (4oz) light soft brown sugar
- 397g (14oz) can sweetened condensed milk
- 150ml (¼pt) double cream
- 2 bananas (sliced)

To decorate: grated milk chocolate or flaky chocolate bar and slices of banana

Chocolate

Bananas

Brown sugar

Equipment
- Food processor or food bag and rolling pin
- Non-stick saucepan
- Wooden spoon • Spoon
- 19cm (7½") loose-bottomed fluted flan tin, 4cm (1½") deep
- Large mixing bowl
- Electric or hand whisk

1 Place the biscuits in a food processor and process until smooth. If you don't have a food processor, place the biscuits in a food bag and crush them with a rolling pin.

2 Melt the butter for the base in a saucepan, then stir in the crushed biscuits with a wooden spoon. Press the mixture into the base and sides of the tin. Chill the base for 30 minutes.

3 Place the diced butter and sugar in the saucepan over a low heat, and stir until the butter has melted. Add the condensed milk and gently bring to the boil, stirring continuously.

4 Boil the butter, sugar and condensed milk for 5 minutes, stirring continuously until it is a pale caramel colour. Pour over the biscuit base and chill for 1 hour.

5 In a large mixing bowl, whip the cream with an electric or hand whisk until it forms soft peaks. Arrange the banana slices over the toffee, then spoon over the whipped cream.

6 Decorate the top of the pie with extra sliced banana and some grated milk chocolate. Serve the pie in slices. Keep chilled and eat within two days.

Strawberry Tartlets

These pretty tartlets taste as good as they look! Make them when the fruit is in season for the best flavour or frozen will also work.

Strawberries

Ingredients

- 225g (8oz) ready-prepared shortcrust pastry
- 150g (5oz) mascarpone cheese
- ½tsp vanilla extract
- 2tbsp icing sugar
- 175g (6oz) strawberries or other soft fruit
- 4tbsp redcurrant jelly
- 15ml (1tbsp) water

Equipment

- Rolling pin
- 9cm (3½") fluted cutter
- 12-hole bun tin
- Eight pieces of aluminium foil
- Oven gloves
- Cooling rack

Bun tin

Mixing bowl

Sieve

Sharp Knife

Oven gloves

- Small mixing bowl
- Wooden spoon
- Sieve
- Chopping board
- Sharp knife
- Teaspoon
- Small saucepan
- Pastry brush

Chopping board

1 Preheat the oven to 200°C (400°F, gas mark 6). Thinly roll out the pastry, then using a 9cm (3½") fluted cutter, cut out eight circles. Press the pastry circles into a bun tin.

2 Press a piece of scrunched-up foil into each case. Cook for 10 minutes, then remove the foil carefully. Return to the oven for 3–4 minutes. Cool in the tin, then transfer to a cooling rack.

3 To make the filling, place the mascarpone cheese and vanilla extract in a small mixing bowl. Sift over the icing sugar, then beat with a wooden spoon until smooth.

Chef's Tip
Placing scrunched up foil in each pastry case prevents them from shrinking.

4 Place the strawberries on a chopping board. Remove the green stalks from the strawberries. Then use a sharp knife to cut them in half. (Quarter them if the strawberries are large.)

5 When the pastry cases are completely cool, use a teaspoon to fill them with the mascarpone and vanilla mixture. Arrange the strawberries over the top.

6 Place the redcurrant jelly in a small pan with the water and cook over a low heat, stirring with a wooden spoon until the jelly has dissolved. Brush this over the strawberries.

Banana Fritters

These bananas are cooked in a light batter, coated with sesame seeds and served with a delicious warm fudge sauce. For extra indulgence add a scoop of vanilla ice cream.

Ingredients

bananas

- 4 bananas, peeled and each cut into 4 pieces
- sunflower oil for frying

Fudge sauce:

- 75g (3oz) unsalted butter
- 150g (5½oz) light soft brown sugar
- 150ml (¼pt) single cream

golden syrup

- 15ml (1tbsp) golden syrup

Batter:

- 125g (4oz) self-raising flour
- 30ml (2tbsp) caster sugar
- 175ml (6floz) milk
- 60ml (4tbsp) sesame seeds

milk

Equipment

- large saucepan
- wooden spoon
- large bowl
- large metal spoon
- teaspoon
- slotted spoon
- kitchen paper

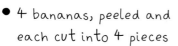
wooden spoon

1 Place all the fudge sauce ingredients in a pan and cook gently for 2 to 3 minutes. Stirring continuously, bring to the boil for 3 minutes, until thickened.

2 Leave in the pan to cool slightly. Meanwhile, heat a pan ⅓ of the volume full of oil, until a piece of bread goes golden brown when dropped in.

3 Mix all the batter ingredients together in a large bowl, reserving 30ml (2tbsp) of the sesame seeds. Add the bananas and turn to coat in the batter.

4 Using a slotted spoon, and holding over the bowl, remove the bananas, then sprinkle with some of the reserved sesame seeds.

5 Fry the banana in batches, in the oil for 3 to 4 minutes until golden brown. Remove and drain on kitchen paper. Serve immediately with the fudge sauce.

These banana fritters are a quick and delicious dessert.

Apple Crumble

In this twist on a classic dessert, apples are cooked in a rich butterscotch sauce, topped with a crunchy, buttery crumble. Serve with custard or ice cream for the ultimate pudding!

Ingredients

- 650g (1½lb) cooking apples
- 75g (3oz) light muscovado sugar
- 25g (1oz) butter
- Finely grated zest and juice ½ lemon
- ¼tsp salt
- 100ml (3½ floz) water

Caster sugar

For the crumble

- 125g (4oz) plain flour
- 75g (3oz) butter (diced)
- 25g (1oz) oats
- 50g (2oz) caster sugar

Lemon

Cooking apples

Plain flour

Butter

Equipment

- Peeler
- Chopping board
- Corer
- Sharp knife
- 900ml (2 pt) ovenproof dish
- Medium saucepan
- Wooden spoon
- Large mixing bowl
- Oven gloves

Corer

Saucepan

1 Preheat the oven to 180°C (350°F, gas mark 4). Using a peeler, peel the apples to remove the skin. Place on a chopping board and use a corer to remove the apple cores.

2 On the chopping board, cut the apples carefully into 2.5cm (1") cube pieces with a sharp knife. Place the pieces in the bottom of an ovenproof dish.

3 Place the sugar, butter, lemon zest and juice and salt in a saucepan with the water. Bring to the boil, stirring occasionally, until the sugar has dissolved and the butter has melted.

Chef's Tip

Don't worry if the butterscotch sauce looks really runny when you pour it over the apples – it will thicken up beautifully in the oven.

4 Pour the butterscotch mixture over the chopped apples in the ovenproof dish and stir with a wooden spoon until the apples are coated evenly in the sauce.

5 Place the flour in a mixing bowl with the diced butter. Using your fingertips, rub in the butter until the mixture looks like rough crumbs. Stir in the oats and the sugar.

6 Spoon the crumble mixture over the top of the apples and bake in the oven on the top shelf for 35–40 minutes until bubbling and golden. Allow to stand for 5 minutes before serving.

Apple Crumble Sundae

Layers of apple, crunchy crumble, toffee sauce and ice cream are layered up in tall glasses to make a delicious sundae, which is a variation on an old favourite.

Helpful Hints

Use good quality vanilla ice cream – your sundaes won't be as delicious if you don't!

Serve these sundaes in traditional sundae glasses for a retro feel.

Ingredients

 cooking apples lemon

Crumble mixture:
- 100g (3½ oz) plain flour
- 50g (2oz) butter (diced)
- 50g (2oz) demerara sugar

Apple compote:
- 3 cooking apples, peeled, cored, and chopped
- 50g (2oz) caster sugar
- juice ½ lemon
- 90ml (8tbsp) cold fudge sauce (see page 200) or ready made toffee sauce
- 8 scoops Vanilla ice cream

Equipment

 bowl

- medium bowl
- baking tray
- baking paper
- medium saucepan
- wooden spoon
- fork

wooden spoon

1 Place the flour and butter in a bowl and rub them together with your fingertips until the mixture resembles fine breadcrumbs. Stir in the sugar.

2 Preheat the oven to 200°C, 400°F, gas mark 6. Line a baking tray with baking paper, and pour the mixture on top. Cook for 8 to 10 minutes until golden.

3 Meanwhile, place the apples, sugar and lemon juice in a medium pan. Cover and cook over a gentle heat for 12 to 15 minutes, stirring occasionally.

4 Leave the apple compote to cool with the lid off. Using your fingers or a fork, break up the cooled crumble topping.

5 Layer each sundae glass with apple compote, crumble, ice cream and toffee sauce and serve with long spoons.

Tasty Twists
Serve warm with ice cream to get a deliciously different dessert!

Marshmallow Squares

These delicious squares of marshmallow and toasted rice are so easy to make and will keep in an airtight container for up to a week.

Ingredients

- 250g (9oz) marshmallows
- 2.5ml (½tsp) vanilla extract
- 100g (3½ oz) butter, diced
- 175g (6oz) toasted rice cereal

toasted rice cereal

Equipment

- 18 x 28cm (7 x 11in) oblong tin
- saucepan
- wooden spoon
- metal spoon
- knife

wooden spoon

saucepan

1 Grease a 18 x 28 cm (7 x 11 in) oblong tin. Place 200g (7oz) of the marshmallows, with the butter and vanilla extract in a medium saucepan.

2 Place over a medium heat and cook until the butter and marshmallows have melted. Roughly chop the remaining marshmallows.

3 Mix the toasted rice with the marshmallow mixture, then stir in the extra marshmallows. Spoon the mixture into the tray and press down with the back of a spoon.

4 Allow to cool in the tray and then cut into squares.

Tasty Twists

Use different coloured marshmallows to make your squares look more colourful.

These are perfect to make if you don't have much time as they are so quick & easy!

Toffee Popcorn

Homemade popcorn is great fun to make and tastes much better than shop-bought.

Tasty Twists

If you prefer salted popcorn, just leave out the toffee sauce and sprinkle over some salt.

Ingredients

- 30ml (2tbsp) corn oil
- 100g (3½ oz) popping corn
- 50g (2oz) butter
- 50g (2oz) soft brown sugar
- 75ml (3tbsp) golden syrup

Equipment

- 2 medium saucepans
- large mixing bowl
- spoon

Wooden spoon

saucepan

1 Heat the oil in a saucepan. Add the corn and, with the lid on, shake to coat in the oil. Over a medium heat, shake the pan occasionally until the corn pops.

2 Remove from the heat. Place the butter, sugar and syrup in another pan. Stir together over a medium heat until the butter has melted and the sugar has dissolved.

3 Put the popcorn into a large mixing bowl and drizzle the toffee sauce over the top.

4 Stir until the popcorn is coated. Stop stirring when the sauce has cooled and is setting. Leave until cool enough to eat.

This recipe makes the perfect accompaniment to your favourite movies!

Helpful Hint

Wait until there are 3 to 5 seconds between each "pop" before you turn off the heat.

Peppermint Creams

These sophisticated sweets make a gorgeous gift for a friend – or maybe for yourself!

Ingredients

icing sugar

- 450g (1lb) icing sugar, sifted
- 120 to 135ml (8 to 9tbsp) sweetened condensed milk
- few drops peppermint extract or essence
- few drops green food colouring
- 150g (5½ oz) plain chocolate

chocolate

rolling pin

Equipment

- mixing bowl
- metal spoon
- rolling pin
- small circular cookie cutter
- baking paper
- heatproof bowl
- saucepan

heatproof bowl

1 Place the icing sugar in a large bowl and add the condensed milk. Stir until you have a crumbly mixture.

2 Add a few drops of the peppermint extract or essence, and a few drops of green food colouring. Knead until you have a smooth firm mixture.

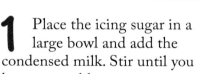
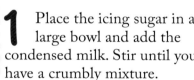

3 Lightly dust the work surface with a little icing sugar and roll out to 5mm (½in) thick. Cut into rounds with a small cutter. Leave to dry on a piece of baking paper.

4 Melt the chocolate in a heatproof bowl over a pan of simmering water, then dip each cream into the melted chocolate. Leave to set.

The combination of chocolate and mint flavours is scrumptious!

Decoration

No cake is complete without some pretty decoration! Whether you use healthy fruit or indulgent icing, here are some top tips for perfect prettiness.

Chef's Tip
Add your liquids, such as water or food colouring, to the icing sugar one drop at a time. You can always add more, but if you add to much it will become too runny.

How to make glacé icing

1 Sift 225g (8oz) icing sugar into a large mixing bowl. You can use your hand or a spoon with the sieve.

2 Gradually stir in 2–3tbsp of hot water. Add a drop of food colouring if you are using it.

How to make buttercream icing

1 Place 75g (3oz) butter in a bowl and beat with a wooden spoon until it has softened.

2 Gradually sift over 175g (6oz) icing sugar. Beat it in with a wooden spoon.

3 Beat in 1–2tbsp milk and/or flavouring until you have a fluffy consistency.

How to make a piping bag

1 Cut out a triangle shape (i.e. half a square) from baking paper. Point the longest side away from you and fold the right hand point over.

2 Fold the left hand point over the cone, bringing all three points together and fold over to secure it in place.

3 Snip off the end with a pair of scissors to create the hole. Put your icing inside the cone and squeeze it out onto the cake. Test it first!

Variation

Here is a selection of cake decorations. They include: sugar strands, sugar flowers, sugar shell chocolate beans and mini-marshmallows.

Glossary

This is the place to find extra information about the cookery words and techniques used in this book.

B

baking blind: weighing down a pastry base with baking beans or foil to stop it from rising during baking.
beat: to stir or mix quickly until smooth, in order to break down or add air.

C

chill: to cool in a refrigerator.
combine: to mix ingredients together.
consistency: how runny or thick a mixture is.
cream: to beat butter and sugar together to add air.
curdle: when the liquid and solid parts of an ingredient or mixture separate. Milk curdles when over-heated and cakes can curdle if the eggs are too cold or added too quickly.

D

dissolve: to melt or liquify a substance (often sugar in water).
drizzle: to pour slowly, in a trickle.
dough: the mixture of flour, water, sugar, salt and yeast (and maybe other ingredients) before it is baked into bread.

E

elastic: a mixture with a stretchy texture.

F

fold: to mix ingredients together gently, to retain as much air in the mixture as possible.
frosting: a topping that is usually a creamy icing.

G

grease: to rub butter onto a baking sheet, tin or tray to prevent the baked item from sticking.

I

individual: a single one, or enough for one person.

K

knead: to press and fold the dough with your hands until it is smooth and stretchy. This distributes the yeast and helps it to rise.

L

level: to make the surface of something the same height.

M

melt: to heat a solid substance until it becomes liquid.
moist: something which is slightly wet.

P

peaks: raised areas that look like the tops of mountains.

preheat: to turn the oven on and heat it to the correct temperature before baking in it.

process: to blend an ingredient or ingredients in a food processor.

Q

quantity: how much of an ingredient you need.

R

rich: strongly flavoured.

ripe: when a fruit is soft and ready to be eaten.

S

savoury: something that does not taste sweet.

serrated: the edge of a knife which has 'teeth'.

sift: to use a sieve to strain a dry ingredient and remove lumps.

simmer: to cook over a low heat so the liquid or food is bubbling gently but not boiling.

sprinkle: to scatter a food lightly over another food.

T

texture: the way something feels, e.g. soft, smooth, chunky, moist, etc.

trimmings: leftover pieces of dough or pastry from cutting out.

W

well: a dip made in some flour in which to crack an egg or pour liquid.

whisk: to evenly mix ingredients together with a whisk.

Y

yeast: a type of fungus that, when added to flour, water, sugar and salt, ferments and causes the mixture to rise.

Z

zest: the skin of a citrus fruit that has been grated with a grater or zester.

Index

Acknowledgements

The publisher would like to thank the following: Young chefs: Shannon Vass and Sophie O'Donohue and assistant Ria Osborne. Photography assistants Jon Cardwell, Michael Hart, and Ria Osborne. The following children for being fantastic hand models and trainee chefs – Latoya Bailey, Efia Brady, Hannah Broom, Ella Bukbardis, Eleanor Bullock, Nakita Clarke, Megan Craddock, Elise Flatman, Eliza Greenslade, George Greenslade, Mykelia Hill, Hannah Leaman, Toby Leaman, Rozina McHugh, Eva Mee, Grace Mee, Louis Moorcraft, Hannah Moore, Shannon O'Kelly, Lily Sansford, Sadie Sansford, Gabriella Soper, Olivia Sullivan-Davis, James Tilley, Rachel Tilley, Charlotte Vogel, and Hope Wadman.

The publisher would like to thank the following for their kind permission to reproduce their photographs:

(Key: a-above; b-below/bottom; c-centre; l-left; r-right; t-top)

iStockphoto.com Ruth Black 8-9; Darren Fisher 2-3; Ivan Mateev 14br; Georgina Palmer 15; Ales Veluscek 18bl; Tomasz Zachariasz 7tr.

Jacket images *Front* **iStockphoto.com** Ruth Black t. *Back* **iStockphoto.com** Mike Sonnenberg bl. *Spine* **iStockphoto.com** Ruth Black bc, cb, t.

All other images © Dorling Kindersley
For further information see: **www.dkimages.com**